JESUS CHRIST THE BEARER OF THE WATER OF LIFE

A CHRISTIAN REFLECTION ON THE 'NEW AGE'

PONTIFICAL COUNCIL FOR CULTURE
PONTIFICAL COUNCIL FOR INTERRELIGIOUS DIALOGUE

All booklets are published thanks to the generous support of the members of the Catholic Truth Society

CATHOLIC TRUTH SOCIETY
PUBLISHERS TO THE HOLY SEE

TABLE OF CONTENTS

FOREWORD

The present study is concerned with the complex phenomenon of '*New Age*' which is influencing many aspects of contemporary culture.

The study is a **provisional report.** It is the fruit of the common reflection of the Working Group on New Religious Movements, composed of staff members of different dicasteries of the Holy See: the Pontifical Councils for Culture and for Interreligious Dialogue (which are the principal redactors for this project), the Congregation for the Evangelisation of Peoples and the Pontifical Council for Promoting Christian Unity.

These reflections are offered primarily to those engaged in pastoral work so that they might be able to explain how the *New Age* movement differs from the Christian faith. This study invites readers to take account of the way that *New Age* religiosity addresses the spiritual hunger of contemporary men and women. It should be recognised that the attraction that *New Age* religiosity has for some Christians may be due in part to the lack of serious attention in their own communities for themes which are actually part of the Catholic synthesis such as the importance of man's spiritual dimension and its integration with the whole of life, the search for life's meaning, the link between human beings and the rest of creation, the desire for personal and social transformation, and the rejection of a rationalistic and materialistic view of humanity.

The present publication calls attention to the need to know and understand *New Age* as a cultural current, as well as the need for Catholics to have an understanding of authentic Catholic doctrine and spirituality in order to properly assess *New Age* themes. The first two chapters present *New Age* as a multifaceted cultural tendency, proposing an analysis of the basic foundations of the thought conveyed in this context. From Chapter Three onwards some indications are offered for an investigation of *New Age* in comparison with the Christian message. Some suggestions of a pastoral nature are also made.

Those who wish to go deeper into the study of *New Age* will find useful references in the appendices. It is hoped that this work will in fact provide a stimulus for further studies adapted to different cultural contexts. Its purpose is also to encourage discernment by those who are looking for sound reference points for a life of greater fulness. It is indeed our conviction that through many of our contemporaries who are searching, we can discover a true thirst for God. As Pope John Paul II said to a group of bishops from the United States: "Pastors must honestly ask whether they have paid sufficient attention to the thirst of the human heart for the true 'living water' which only Christ our Redeemer can give (cf. *Jn* 4:7-13)". Like him, we want to rely on the perennial freshness of the Gospel message and its capacity to transform and renew those who accept it" (*AAS* 86/4, 330).

1. WHAT SORT OF REFLECTION?

The following reflections are meant as a guide for Catholics involved in preaching the Gospel and teaching the faith at any level within the Church. This document does not aim at providing a set of complete answers to the many questions raised by the *New Age* or other contemporary signs of the perennial human search for happiness, meaning and salvation. It is an invitation to understand the *New Age* and to engage in a genuine dialogue with those who are influenced by *New Age* thought. The document guides those involved in pastoral work in their understanding and response to *New Age* spirituality, both illustrating the points where this spirituality contrasts with the Catholic faith and refuting the positions espoused by *New Age* thinkers in opposition to Christian faith. What is indeed required of Christians is, first and foremost, a solid grounding in their faith. On this sound base, they can build a life which responds positively to the invitation in the first letter of Saint Peter: "always have your answer ready for people who ask you the reason for the hope that you all have. But give it with courtesy and respect and a clear conscience" (*1 P* 3:15 f).

1.1. Why now?

The beginning of the Third Millennium comes not only two thousand years after the birth of Christ, but also at a time when astrologers believe that the Age of Pisces - known to them as the Christian age - is drawing to a close. These reflections are about the *New Age*, which takes its name from the imminent astrological Age of Aquarius. The *New Age* is one of many explanations of the significance of this moment in history which are bombarding contemporary (particularly western) culture, and it is hard to see clearly what is and what is not consistent with the Christian message. So this seems to be the right moment to offer a Christian assessment of *New Age* thinking and the *New Age* movement as a whole.

It has been said, quite correctly, that many people hover between certainty and uncertainty these days, particularly in questions relating to their identity.[1] Some say that the Christian religion is patriarchal and authoritarian, that political institutions are unable to improve the world, and that formal (allopathic) medicine simply fails to heal people effectively. The fact that what were once central elements in society are now perceived as untrustworthy or lacking in genuine authority has created a climate where people look inwards, into themselves, for meaning and strength. There is also a search for alternative institutions, which people hope will respond to their deepest needs. The unstructured or chaotic life of alternative communities of the 1970s has given way to a search for discipline and structures, which are clearly key elements in the immensely popular 'mystical' movements. *New Age* is attractive mainly because so much of what it offers meets hungers often left unsatisfied by the established institutions.

While much of *New Age* is a reaction to contemporary culture, there are many ways in which it is that culture's child. The Renaissance and the Reformation have shaped the modern western individual, who is not weighed down by external burdens like merely extrinsic authority and tradition; people feel the need to 'belong' to institutions less and less (and yet loneliness is very much a scourge of modern life), and are not inclined to rank 'official' judgements above their own. With this cult of humanity, religion is internalised in a way which prepares the ground for a celebration of the sacredness of the self. This is why *New Age* shares many of the values espoused by enterprise culture and the 'prosperity Gospel' (of which more will be said later: section 2.4), and also by the consumer culture, whose influence is clear from the rapidly-growing numbers of people who claim that it is possible to blend Christianity and *New Age*, by taking what strikes them as the best of both.[2] It is worth remembering that deviations within Christianity have also gone beyond traditional theism in accepting a unilateral turn to self, and this would encourage such a blending of approaches. The important thing to note is that God is reduced in certain *New Age* practices so as furthering the advancement of the individual.

---

[1] Paul Heelas, *The New Age Movement. The Celebration of the Self and the Sacralization of Modernity*, Oxford (Blackwell) 1996, p. 137.
[2] Cf. P. Heelas, *op. cit.*, p. 164f.

New Age appeals to people imbued with the values of modern culture. Freedom, authenticity, self-reliance and the like are all held to be sacred. It appeals to those who have problems with patriarchy. It "does not demand any more faith or belief than going to the cinema",[3] and yet it claims to satisfy people's spiritual appetites. But here is a central question: just what is meant by spirituality in a *New Age* context? The answer is the key to unlocking some of the differences between the Christian tradition and much of what can be called *New Age*. Some versions of *New Age* harness the powers of nature and seek to communicate with another world to discover the fate of individuals, to help individuals tune in to the right frequency to make the most of themselves and their circumstances. In most cases, it is completely fatalistic. Christianity, on the other hand, is an invitation to look outwards and beyond, to the 'new Advent' of the God who calls us to live the dialogue of love.[4]

1.2. Communications

The technological revolution in communications over the last few years has brought about a completely new situation. The ease and speed with which people can now communicate is one of the reasons why *New Age* has come to the attention of people of all ages and backgrounds, and many who follow Christ are not sure what it is all about. The Internet, in particular, has become enormously influential, especially with younger people, who find it a congenial and fascinating way of acquiring information. But it is a volatile vehicle of misinformation on so many aspects of religion: not all that is labelled 'Christian' or 'Catholic' can be trusted to reflect the teachings of the Catholic Church and, at the same time, there is a remarkable expansion of *New Age* sources ranging from the serious to the ridiculous. People need, and have a right to, reliable information on the differences between Christianity and *New Age*.

---

[3]Cf. P. Heelas, *op. cit.*, p. 173.
[4]Cf. John Paul II, Encyclical Letter *Dominum et vivificantem* (18 May 1986), 53.

1.3. Cultural background

When one examines many *New Age* traditions, it soon becomes clear that there is, in fact, little in the *New Age* that is new. The name seems to have gained currency through Rosicrucianism and Freemasonry, at the time of the French and American Revolutions, but the reality it denotes is a contemporary variant of Western esotericism. This dates back to Gnostic groups which grew up in the early days of Christianity, and gained momentum at the time of the Reformation in Europe. It has grown in parallel with scientific world-views, and acquired a rational justification through the eighteenth and nineteenth centuries. It has involved a progressive rejection of a personal God and a focus on other entities which would often figure as intermediaries between God and humanity in traditional Christianity, with more and more original adaptations of these or additional ones. A powerful trend in modern Western culture which has given space to *New Age* ideas is the general acceptance of Darwinist evolutionary theory; this, alongside a focus on hidden spiritual powers or forces in nature, has been the backbone of much of what is now recognised as *New Age* theory. Basically, *New Age* has found a remarkable level of acceptance because the world-view on which it was based was already widely accepted. The ground was well prepared by the growth and spread of relativism, along with an antipathy or indifference towards the Christian faith. Furthermore, there has been a lively discussion about whether and in what sense *New Age* can be described as a postmodern phenomenon. The existence and fervour of *New Age* thinking and practice bear witness to the unquenchable longing of the human spirit for transcendence and religious meaning, which is not only a contemporary cultural phenomenon, but was evident in the ancient world, both Christian and pagan.

1.4. The *New Age* and Catholic Faith

Even if it can be admitted that *New Age* religiosity in some way responds to the legitimate spiritual longing of human nature, it must be acknowledged that its attempts to do so run counter to Christian revelation. In Western culture in particular, the appeal of 'alternative' approaches to spirituality is very strong. On the one hand, new forms of psychological affirmation of the individual have become very popular among Catholics, even in retreat-houses, seminaries and institutes of formation for religious. At the same time there is increasing nostalgia and curiosity for the wisdom and ritual of long ago, which is one of the reasons for the remarkable growth in the popularity of esotericism and gnosticism. Many people are particularly attracted to what is known - correctly or otherwise - as 'Celtic' spirituality,[5] or to the religions of ancient peoples. Books and courses on spirituality and ancient or Eastern religions are a booming business, and they are frequently labelled '*New Age*' for commercial purposes. But the links with those religions are not always clear. In fact, they are often denied.

An adequate Christian discernment of *New Age* thought and practice cannot fail to recognise that, like second and third century gnosticism, it represents something of a compendium of positions that the Church has identified as heterodox. John Paul II warns with regard to the "return of ancient gnostic ideas under the guise of the so-called *New Age:* We cannot delude ourselves that this will lead toward a renewal of religion. It is only a new way of practising gnosticism - that attitude of the spirit that, in the name of a profound knowledge of God, results in distorting His Word and replacing it with purely human words. Gnosticism never completely abandoned the realm of Christianity. Instead, it has always existed side by side with Christianity, sometimes taking the shape of a philosophical movement, but more often assuming the characteristics of a religion or a para-religion in distinct, if not declared, conflict with all that is essentially Christian".[6] An example of this can be seen in the enneagram, the nine-type tool for character analysis, which when used as a means of spiritual growth introduces an ambiguity in the doctrine and the life of the Christian faith.

---

[5]Cf. Gilbert Markus o.p., "Celtic Schmeltic", (1) in *Spirituality*, vol. 4, November-December 1998, No 21, pp. 379-383 and (2) in *Spirituality,* vol. 5, January-February 1999, No. 22, pp. 57-61.

[6]John Paul II, *Crossing the Threshold of Hope,* (Knopf) 1994, 90.

1.5. A positive challenge

The appeal of *New Age* religiosity cannot be underestimated. When the understanding of the content of Christian faith is weak, some mistakenly hold that the Christian religion does not inspire a profound spirituality and so they seek elsewhere. As a matter of fact, some say the *New Age* is already passing us by, and refer to the 'next' age.[7] They speak of a crisis that began to manifest itself in the United States of America in the early 1990s, but admit that, especially beyond the English-speaking world, such a 'crisis' may come later. But bookshops and radio stations, and the plethora of self-help groups in so many Western towns and cities, all seem to tell a different story. It seems that, at least for the moment, the *New Age* is still very much alive and part of the current cultural scene.

The success of *New Age* offers the Church a challenge. People feel the Christian religion no longer offers them - or perhaps never gave them - something they really need. The search which often leads people to the *New Age* is a genuine yearning: for a deeper spirituality, for something which will touch their hearts, and for a way of making sense of a confusing and often alienating world. There is a positive tone in *New Age* criticisms of "the materialism of daily life, of philosophy and even of medicine and psychiatry; reductionism, which refuses to take into consideration religious and supernatural experiences; the industrial culture of unrestrained individualism, which teaches egoism and pays no attention to other people, the future and the environment".[8] Any problems there are with *New Age* are to be found in what it proposes as alternative answers to life's questions. If the Church is not to be accused of being deaf to people's longings, her members need to do two things: to root themselves ever more firmly in the fundamentals of their faith, and to understand the often-silent cry in people's hearts, which leads them elsewhere if they are not satisfied by the Church. There is also a call in all of this to come closer to Jesus Christ and to be ready to follow Him, since He is the real way to happiness, the truth about God and the fulness of life for every man and woman who is prepared to respond to his love.

---

[7]Cf. particularly Massimo Introvigne, *New Age & Next Age,* Casale Monferrato (Piemme) 2000.
[8]M. Introvigne, *op. cit.,* p. 267.

2. *NEW AGE* SPIRITUALITY: AN OVERVIEW

Christians in many Western societies, and increasingly also in other parts of the world, frequently come into contact with different aspects of the phenomenon known as *New Age*. Many of them feel the need to understand how they can best approach something which is at once so alluring, complex, elusive and, at times, disturbing. These reflections are an attempt to help Christians do two things:

- to identify elements of the developing *New Age* tradition;
- to indicate those elements which are inconsistent with the Christian revelation.

This is a pastoral response to a current challenge, which does not even attempt to provide an exhaustive list of *New Age* phenomena, since that would result in a very bulky tome, and such information is readily available elsewhere. It is essential to try to understand *New Age* correctly, in order to evaluate it fairly, and avoid creating a caricature. It would be unwise and untrue to say that everything connected with the *New Age* movement is good, or that everything about it is bad. Nevertheless, given the underlying vision of *New Age* religiosity, it is on the whole difficult to reconcile it with Christian doctrine and spirituality.

New Age is not a movement in the sense normally intended in the term 'New Religious Movement', and it is not what is normally meant by the terms 'cult' and 'sect'. Because it is spread across cultures, in phenomena as varied as music, films, seminars, workshops, retreats, therapies, and many more activities and events, it is much more diffuse and informal, though some religious or para-religious groups consciously incorporate *New Age* elements, and it has been suggested that *New Age* has been a source of ideas for various religious and para-religious sects.[9] *New Age* is not a single, uniform movement, but rather a loose network of practitioners whose approach is to

[9]Cf. Michel Lacroix, *L'Ideologia della New Age,* Milano (il Saggiatore) 1998, p. 86. The word 'sect' is used here not in any pejorative sense, but rather to denote a sociological phenomenon.

think globally but act locally. People who are part of the network do not necessarily know each other and rarely, if ever, meet. In an attempt to avoid the confusion which can arise from using the term 'movement', some refer to *New Age* as a 'milieu',[10] or an 'audience cult'.[11] However, it has also been pointed out that "it is a very coherent current of thought",[12] a deliberate challenge to modern culture. It is a syncretistic structure incorporating many diverse elements, allowing people to share interests or connections to very different degrees and on varying levels of commitment. Many trends, practices and attitudes which are in some way part of *New Age* are, indeed, part of a broad and readily identifiable reaction to mainstream culture, so the word 'movement' is not entirely out of place. It can be applied to *New Age* in the same sense as it is to other broad social movements, like the Civil Rights movement or the Peace Movement; like them, it includes a bewildering array of people linked to the movement's main aims, but very diverse in the way they are involved and in their understanding of particular issues.

The expression '*New Age* religion' is more controversial, so it seems best to avoid it, although *New Age* is often a response to people's religious questions and needs, and its appeal is to people who are trying to discover or rediscover a spiritual dimension in their life. Avoidance of the term '*New Age* religion' is not meant in any way to question the genuine character of people's search for meaning and sense in life; it respects the fact that many within the *New Age* Movement themselves distinguish carefully between 'religion' and 'spirituality'. Many have rejected organised religion, because in their judgement it has failed to answer their needs, and for precisely this reason they have looked elsewhere to find 'spirituality'. Furthermore, at the heart of *New Age* is the belief that the time for particular religions is over, so to refer to it as a religion would run counter to its own self-understanding. However, it is

---

[10]Cf. Wouter J. Hanegraaff, *New Age Religion and Western Culture. Esotericism in the Mirror of Secular Thought,* Leiden-New York-Köln (Brill) 1996, p. 377 and elsewhere.

[11]Cf. Rodney Stark and William Sims Bainbridge, *The Future of Religion. Secularisation, Revival and Cult Formation,* Berkeley (University of California Press) 1985.

[12]Cf. M. Lacroix, *op. cit.,* p. 8.

quite accurate to place *New Age* in the broader context of esoteric religiousness, whose appeal continues to grow.[13]

There is a problem built into the current text. It is an attempt to understand and evaluate something which is basically an exaltation of the richness of human experience. It is bound to draw the criticism that it can never do justice to a cultural movement whose essence is precisely to break out of what are seen as the constricting limits of rational discourse. But it is meant as an invitation to Christians to take the *New Age* seriously, and as such asks its readers to enter into a critical dialogue with people approaching the same world from very different perspectives.

The pastoral effectiveness of the Church in the Third Millennium depends to a great extent on the preparation of effective communicators of the Gospel message. What follows is a response to the difficulties expressed by many in dealing with the very complex and elusive phenomenon known as *New Age*. It is an attempt to understand what *New Age* is and to recognise the questions to which it claims to offer answers and solutions. There are some excellent books and other resources which survey the whole phenomenon or explain particular aspects in great detail, and reference will be made to some of these in the appendix. However they do not always undertake the necessary discernment in the light of Christian faith. The purpose of this contribution is to help Catholics find a key to understanding the basic principles behind *New Age* thinking, so that they can then make a Christian evaluation of the elements of *New Age* they encounter. It is worth saying that many people dislike the term *New Age*, and some suggest that 'alternative spirituality' may be more correct and less limiting. It is also true that many of the phenomena mentioned in this document will probably not bear any particular label, but it is presumed, for the sake of brevity, that readers will recognise a phenomenon or set of phenomena that can justifiably at least be linked with the general cultural movement that is often known as *New Age*.

---

[13]The Swiss "Theologie für Laien" course entitled *Faszination Esoterik* puts this clearly. Cf. "Kursmappe 1 - *New Age* und Esoterik", text to accompany slides, p. 9.

2.1. What is new about *New Age*?

For many people, the term *New Age* clearly refers to a momentous turning-point in history. According to astrologers, we live in the Age of Pisces, which has been dominated by Christianity. But the current age of Pisces is due to be replaced by the *New Age* of Aquarius early in the third Millennium.[14] The Age of Aquarius has such a high profile in the *New Age* movement largely because of the influence of theosophy, spiritualism and anthroposophy, and their esoteric antecedents. People who stress the imminent change in the world are often expressing a *wish* for such a change, not so much in the world itself as in our culture, in the way we relate to the world; this is particularly clear in those who stress the idea of a New Paradigm for living. It is an attractive approach since, in some of its expressions, people do not watch passively, but have an active role in changing culture and bringing about a new spiritual awareness. In other expressions, more power is ascribed to the inevitable progression of natural cycles. In any case, the Age of Aquarius is a vision, not a theory. But *New Age* is a broad tradition, which incorporates many ideas which have no explicit link with the change from the Age of Pisces to the Age of Aquarius. There are moderate, but quite generalised, visions of a future where there will be a planetary spirituality alongside separate religions, similar planetary political institutions to complement more local ones, global economic entities which are more participatory and democratic, greater emphasis on communication and education, a mixed approach to health combining professional medicine and self-healing, a more androgynous self-understanding and ways of integrating science, mysticism, technology and ecology. Again, this is evidence of a deep desire for a fulfilling and healthy existence for the human race and for the planet. Some of the traditions which flow into *New Age* are: ancient Egyptian occult practices, Cabbalism, early Christian gnosticism, Sufism, the lore of the

[14]The term was already in use in the title of *The New Age Magazine,* which was being published by the Ancient Accepted Scottish Masonic Rite in the southern jurisdiction of the United States of America as early as 1900 Cf. M. York, "The *New Age* Movement in Great Britain", in *Syzygy. Journal of Alternative Religion and Culture,* 1: 2-3 (1992), Stanford CA, p. 156, note 6. The exact timing and nature of the change to the New Age are interpreted variously by different authors; estimates of timing range from 1967 to 2376.

Druids, Celtic Christianity, mediaeval alchemy, Renaissance hermeticism, Zen Buddhism, Yoga and so on.[15]

Here is what is 'new' about *New Age*. It is a "syncretism of esoteric and secular elements".[16] They link into a widely-held perception that the time is ripe for a fundamental change in individuals, in society and in the world. There are various expressions of the need for a shift:

- from Newtonian mechanistic physics to quantum physics;
- from modernity's exaltation of reason to an appreciation of feeling, emotion and experience (often described as a switch from 'left brain' *rational* thinking to 'right brain' *intuitive* thinking);
- from a dominance of masculinity and patriarchy to a celebration of femininity, in individuals and in society.

In these contexts the term 'paradigm shift' is often used. In some cases it is clearly supposed that this shift is not simply desirable, but inevitable. The rejection of modernity underlying this desire for change is not new, but can be described as "a modern revival of pagan religions with a mixture of influences from both eastern religions and also from modern psychology, philosophy, science, and the counterculture that developed in the 1950s and 1960s".[17] *New Age* is a witness to nothing less than a cultural revolution, a complex reaction to the dominant ideas and values in western culture, and yet its idealistic criticism is itself ironically typical of the culture it criticises.

A word needs to be said on the notion of *paradigm shift*. It was made popular by Thomas Kuhn, an American historian of science,

[15] In late 1977, Marilyn Ferguson sent a questionnaire to 210 "persons engaged in social transformation", whom she also calls "Aquarian Conspirators". The following is interesting: "When respondents were asked to name individuals whose ideas had influenced them, either through personal contact or through their writings, those most often named, in order of frequency, were Pierre Teilhard de Chardin, C.G. Jung, Abraham Maslow, Carl Rogers, Aldous Huxley, Robert Assagioli, and J. Krishnamurti. "Others frequently mentioned: Paul Tillich, Hermann Hesse, Alfred North Whitehead, Martin Buber, Ruth Benedict, Margaret Mead, Gregory Bateson, Tarthang Tulku, Alan Watts, Sri Aurobindo, Swami Muktananda, D.T. Suzuki, Thomas Merton, Willis Harman, Kenneth Boulding, Elise Boulding, Erich Fromm, Marshall McLuhan, Buckminster Fuller, Frederic Spiegelberg, Alfred Korzybski, Heinz von Foerster, John Lilly, Werner Erhard, Oscar Ichazo, Maharishi Mahesh Yogi, Joseph Chilton Pearce, Karl Pribram, Gardner Murphy, and Albert Einstein": *The Aquarian Conspiracy. Personal and Social Transformation in Our Time,* Los Angeles (Tarcher) 1980, p. 50 (note 1) and p. 434.

[16] W.J. Hanegraaff, *op. cit.*, p. 520.

[17] Irish Theological Commission, *A New Age of the Spirit? A Catholic Response to the New Age Phenomenon,* Dublin 1994, chapter 3.

who saw a paradigm as "the entire constellation of beliefs, values, techniques and so on shared by the members of a given community".[18] When there is a shift from one paradigm to another, it is a question of wholesale transformation of perspective rather than one of gradual development. It really is a revolution, and Kuhn emphasised that competing paradigms are incommensurable and cannot co-exist. So the idea that a paradigm shift in the area of religion and spirituality is simply a new way of stating traditional beliefs misses the point. What is actually going on is a radical change in world-view, which puts into question not only the content but also the fundamental interpretation of the former vision. Perhaps the clearest example of this, in terms of the relationship between *New Age* and Christianity, is the total recasting of the life and significance of Jesus Christ. It is impossible to reconcile these two visions.[19]

Science and technology have clearly failed to deliver all they once seemed to promise, so in their search for meaning and liberation people have turned to the spiritual realm. *New Age* as we now know it came from a search for something more humane and beautiful than the oppressive, alienating experience of life in Western society. Its early exponents were prepared to look far afield in their search, so it has become a very eclectic approach. It may well be one of the signs of a 'return to religion', but it is most certainly not a return to orthodox Christian doctrines and creeds. The first symbols of this 'movement' to penetrate Western culture were the remarkable festival at Woodstock in New York State in 1969 and the musical *Hair*, which set forth the main themes of *New Age* in the emblematic song 'Aquarius'.[20] But these were merely the tip of an iceberg whose dimensions have become clearer only relatively recently. The idealism of the 1960s and 1970s still survives in some quarters; but now, it is no longer predominantly adolescents who are involved.

---

[18]Cf. *The Structure of Scientific Revolutions,* Chicago (University of Chicago Press), 1970, p. 175.

[19]Cf. Alessandro Olivieri Pennesi, *Il Cristo del New Age. Indagine critica,* Vatican City (Libreria Editrice Vaticana) 1999, *passim,* but especially pp. 11-34. See Also section 4 below.

[20]It is worth recalling the lyrics of this song, which quickly imprinted themselves on to the minds of a whole generation in North America and Western Europe: "When the Moon is in the Seventh House, and Jupiter aligns with Mars, then Peace will guide the Planets, and Love will steer the Stars. This is the dawning of the Age of Aquarius... Harmony and understanding, sympathy and trust abounding; no more falsehoods or derision - golden living, dreams of visions, mystic crystal revelation, and the mind's true liberation. Aquarius...".

Links with left-wing political ideology have faded, and psychedelic drugs are by no means as prominent as they once were. So much has happened since then that all this no longer seems revolutionary; 'spiritual' and 'mystical' tendencies formerly restricted to the counterculture are now an established part of mainstream culture, affecting such diverse facets of life as medicine, science, art and religion. Western culture is now imbued with a more general political and ecological awareness, and this whole cultural shift has had an enormous impact on people's life-styles. It is suggested by some that the *New Age* 'movement' is precisely this major change to what is reckoned to be "a significantly better way of life".[21]

2.2. What does the *New Age* claim to offer?

2.2.1. Enchantment: There Must be an Angel

One of the most common elements in *New Age* 'spirituality' is a fascination with extraordinary manifestations, and in particular with paranormal entities. People recognised as 'mediums' claim that their personality is taken over by another entity during trances in a *New Age* phenomenon known as 'channeling', during which the medium may lose control over his or her body and faculties. Some people who have witnessed these events would willingly acknowledge that the manifestations are indeed spiritual, but are not from God, despite the language of love and light which is almost always used... It is probably more correct to refer to this as a contemporary form of spiritualism, rather than spirituality in a strict sense. Other friends and counsellors from the spirit world are angels (which have become the centre of a new industry of books and paintings). Those who refer to angels in the *New Age* do so in an unsystematic way; in fact, distinctions in this area are sometimes described as unhelpful if they are too precise, since "there are many levels of guides, entities, energies, and beings in every octave of the universe... They are all there to pick and choose from in

---

[21] P. Heelas, op. cit., p. 1f. The August 1978 journal of the Berkeley Christian Coalition puts it this way: "Just ten years ago the funky drug-based spirituality of the hippies and the mysticism of the Western yogi were restricted to the counterculture. Today, both have found their way into the mainstream of our cultural mentality. Science, the health professions, and the arts, not to mention psychology and religion, are all engaged in a fundamental reconstruction of their basic premises". Quoted in Marilyn Ferguson, *op. cit.*, p. 370f.

relation to your own attraction/repulsion mechanisms".[22] These spiritual entities are often invoked 'non-religiously' to help in relaxation aimed at better decision-making and control of one's life and career. Fusion with some spirits who teach through particular people is another *New Age* experience claimed by people who refer to themselves as 'mystics'. Some nature spirits are described as powerful energies existing in the natural world and also on the 'inner planes': i.e. those which are accessible by the use of rituals, drugs and other techniques for reaching altered states of consciousness. It is clear that, in theory at least, the *New Age* often recognises no spiritual authority higher than personal inner experience.

2.2.2. Harmony and Understanding: Good Vibrations

Phenomena as diverse as the Findhorn garden and *Feng Shui*[23] represent a variety of ways which illustrate the importance of being in tune with nature or the cosmos. In *New Age* there is no distinction between good and evil. Human actions are the fruit of either illumination or ignorance. Hence we cannot condemn anyone, and nobody needs forgiveness. Believing in the existence of evil can create only negativity and fear. The answer to negativity is *love*. But it is not the sort which has to be translated into deeds; it is more a question of attitudes of mind. Love is energy, a high-frequency vibration, and the secret to happiness and health and success is being able to tune in, to find one's place in the great chain of being. *New Age* teachers and therapies claim to offer the key to finding the correspondences between all the elements of the universe, so that people may modulate the tone of their lives and be in absolute harmony with each other and with everything around them, although there are different theoretical backgrounds.[24]

---

[22]Cf. Chris Griscom, *Ecstasy is a New Frequency: Teachings of the Light Institute,* New York (Simon & Schuster) 1987, p. 82.

[23]See the Glossary of *New Age* terms, §7.2 above.

[24]Cf. W.J. Hanegraaff, *op. cit.,* chapter 15 ("The Mirror of Secular Thought"). The system of correspondences is clearly inherited from traditional esotericism, but it has a new meaning for those who (consciously or not) follow Swedenborg. While every natural element in traditional esoteric doctrine had the divine life within it, for Swedenborg nature is a dead reflection of the living spiritual world. This idea is very much at the heart of the post-modern vision of a disenchanted world and various attempts to 're-enchant' it. Blavatsky rejected correspondences, and Jung emphatically relativised causality in favour of the esoteric world-view of correspondences.

2.2.3. Health: Golden living

Formal (allopathic) medicine today tends to limit itself to curing particular, isolated ailments, and fails to look at the broader picture of a person's health: this has given rise to a fair amount of understandable dissatisfaction. Alternative therapies have gained enormously in popularity because they claim to look at the whole person and are about *healing* rather than *curing*. Holistic health, as it is known, concentrates on the important role that the mind plays in physical healing. The connection between the spiritual and the physical aspects of the person is said to be in the immune system or the Indian chakra system. In a *New Age* perspective, illness and suffering come from working against nature; when one is in tune with nature, one can expect a much healthier life, and even material prosperity; for some *New Age* healers, there should actually be no need for us to die. Developing our human potential will put us in touch with our inner divinity, and with those parts of ourselves which have been alienated and suppressed. This is revealed above all in Altered States of Consciousness (ASCs), which are induced either by drugs or by various mind-expanding techniques, particularly in the context of 'transpersonal psychology'. The shaman is often seen as the specialist of altered states of consciousness, one who is able to mediate between the transpersonal realms of spirits and gods and the world of humans.

There is a remarkable variety of approaches for promoting holistic health, some derived from ancient cultural traditions, whether religious or esoteric, others connected with the psychological theories developed in Esalen during the years 1960-1970. Advertising connected with *New Age* covers a wide range of practices as acupuncture, biofeedback, chiropractic, kinesiology, homeopathy, iridology, massage and various kinds of 'bodywork' (such as orgonomy, Feldenkrais, reflexology, Rolfing, polarity massage, therapeutic touch etc.), meditation and visualisation, nutritional therapies, psychic healing, various kinds of herbal medicine, healing by crystals, metals, music or colours, reincarnation therapies and, finally, twelve-step programmes and self-help groups.[25] The source of healing is said to be within ourselves, something we reach when we are in touch with our inner energy or cosmic energy.

Inasmuch as health includes a prolongation of life, *New Age* offers an Eastern formula in Western terms. Originally, reincarnation was a part of Hindu cyclical thought, based on the *atman* or divine kernel of personality (later the concept of *jiva*), which moved from body to body in a cycle of suffering (*samsara*), determined by the law of *karma*, linked to behaviour in past lives. Hope lies in the possibility of being born into a better state, or ultimately in liberation from the need to be reborn. What is different in most Buddhist traditions is that what wanders from body to body is not a soul, but a continuum of consciousness. Present life is embedded in a potentially endless cosmic process which includes even the gods. In the West, since the time of Lessing, reincarnation has been understood far more optimistically as a process of learning and progressive individual fulfilment. Spiritualism, theosophy, anthroposophy and *New Age* all see reincarnation as participation in cosmic evolution. This post-Christian approach to eschatology is said to answer the unresolved questions of theodicy and dispenses with the notion of hell. When the soul is separated from the body individuals can look back on their whole life up to that point, and when the soul is united to its new body there is a preview of its coming phase of life. People have access to their former lives through dreams and meditation techniques.[26]

2.2.4. Wholeness: A Magical Mystery Tour

One of the central concerns of the *New Age* movement is the search for 'wholeness'. There is encouragement to overcome all forms of 'dualism', as such divisions are an unhealthy product of a less enlightened past. Divisions which *New Age* proponents claim need to be overcome include the real difference between Creator and

---

[25]W.J. Hanegraaff, *op. cit.*, pp. 54-55.

[26]Cf. Reinhard Hümmel, "Reinkarnation", in Hans Gasper, Joachim Müller, Friederike Valentin (eds.), *Lexikon der Sekten, Sondergruppen und Weltanschauungen. Fakten, Hintergründe, Klärungen*, Freiburg-Basel-Wien (Herder) 2000, 886-893.

creation, the real distinction between man and nature, or spirit and matter, which are all considered wrongly as forms of dualism. These dualistic tendencies are often assumed to be ultimately based on the Judaeo-Christian roots of western civilisation, while it would be more accurate to link them to gnosticism, in particular to Manichaeism. The scientific revolution and the spirit of modern rationalism are blamed particularly for the tendency to fragmentation, which treats organic wholes as mechanisms that can be reduced to their smallest components and then explained in terms of the latter, and the tendency to reduce spirit to matter, so that spiritual reality - including the soul - becomes merely a contingent 'epiphenomenon' of essentially material processes. In all of these areas, the *New Age* alternatives are called 'holistic'. Holism pervades the *New Age* movement, from its concern with holistic health to its quest for unitive consciousness, and from ecological awareness to the idea of global 'networking'.

2.3. The fundamental principles of *New Age* thinking

2.3.1. A global response in a time of crisis

"Both the Christian tradition and the secular faith in an unlimited process of science had to face a severe break first manifested in the student revolutions around the year 1968".[27] The wisdom of older generations was suddenly robbed of significance and respect, while the omnipotence of science evaporated, so that the Church now "has to face a serious breakdown in the transmission of her faith to the younger generation".[28] A general loss of faith in these former pillars of consciousness and social cohesion has been accompanied by the unexpected return of cosmic religiosity, rituals and beliefs which many believed to have been supplanted by Christianity; but this perennial esoteric undercurrent never really went away. The surge in popularity of Asian religion at this point was something new in the Western context, established late in the nineteenth century in the theosophical movement, and it "reflects the growing

[27] Michael Fuss, "New Age and Europe - A Challenge for Theology", in *Mission Studies* Vol. VIII-2, 16, 1991, p. 192.

[28] *Ibid., loc. cit.*

awareness of a global spirituality, incorporating all existing religious traditions".[29]

The perennial philosophical question of the one and the many has its modern and contemporary form in the temptation to overcome not only undue division, but even real difference and distinction, and the most common expression of this is holism, an essential ingredient in *New Age* and one of the principal signs of the times in the last quarter of the twentieth century. An extraordinary amount of energy has gone into the effort to overcome the division into compartments characteristic of mechanistic ideology, but this has led to the sense of obligation to submit to a global network which assumes quasi-transcendental authority. Its clearest implications are a process of conscious transformation and the development of ecology.[30] The new vision which is the goal of conscious transformation has taken time to formulate, and its enactment is resisted by older forms of thought judged to be entrenched in the status quo. What has been successful is the generalisation of ecology as a fascination with nature and resacralisation of the earth, Mother Earth or *Gaia*, with the missionary zeal characteristic of Green politics. The Earth's executive agent is the human race as a whole, and the *harmony and understanding* required for responsible governance is increasingly understood to be a global government, with a global ethical framework. The warmth of Mother Earth, whose divinity pervades the whole of creation, is held to bridge the gap between creation and the transcendent Father-God of Judaism and Christianity, and removes the prospect of being judged by such a Being.

In such a vision of a closed universe that contains 'God' and other spiritual beings along with ourselves, we recognise here an implicit pantheism. This is a fundamental point which pervades all *New Age* thought and practice, and conditions in advance any otherwise positive assessment where we might be in favour of one or another aspect of its spirituality. As Christians, we believe on the contrary that "man is essentially a creature and remains so for all

[29]*Ibid.*, p. 193.
[30]*Ibid.*, p. 199.

eternity, so that an absorption of the human I in the divine I will never be possible".[31]

2.3.2. The essential matrix of New Age thinking

The essential matrix of *New Age* thinking is to be found in the esoteric-theosophical tradition which was fairly widely accepted in European intellectual circles in the 18th and 19th centuries. It was particularly strong in freemasonry, spiritualism, occultism and theosophy, which shared a kind of esoteric culture. In this world-view, the visible and invisible universes are linked by a series of correspondences, analogies and influences between microcosm and macrocosm, between metals and planets, between planets and the various parts of the human body, between the visible cosmos and the invisible realms of reality. Nature is a living being, shot through with networks of sympathy and antipathy, animated by a light and a secret fire which human beings seek to control. People can contact the upper or lower worlds by means of their imagination (an organ of the soul or spirit), or by using mediators (angels, spirits, devils) or rituals.

People can be initiated into the mysteries of the cosmos, God and the self by means of a spiritual itinerary of transformation. The eventual goal is *gnosis*, the highest form of knowledge, the equivalent of salvation. It involves a search for the oldest and highest tradition in philosophy (what is inappropriately called *philosophia perennis*) and religion (primordial theology), a secret (esoteric) doctrine which is the key to all the 'exoteric' traditions which are accessible to everyone. Esoteric teachings are handed down from master to disciple in a gradual programme of initiation.

19th century esotericism is seen by some as completely secularised. Alchemy, magic, astrology and other elements of traditional esotericism had been thoroughly integrated with aspects of modern culture, including the search for causal laws, evolutionism, psychology and the study of religions. It reached its clearest form in the ideas of Helena Blavatsky, a Russian medium who founded the *Theosophical Society* with Henry Olcott in New

[31] Congregation for the Doctrine of Faith, *Letter to the Bishops of the Catholic Church on Some Aspects of Christian Meditation (Orationis Formas)*, 1989, 14. Cf. *Gaudium et Spes*, 19; *Fides et Ratio*, 22.

York in 1875. The Society aimed to fuse elements of Eastern and Western traditions in an evolutionary type of spiritualism. It had three main aims:

1. "To form a nucleus of the Universal Brotherhood of Humanity, without distinction of race, creed, caste or colour.
2. "To encourage the study of comparative religion, philosophy and science.
3. "To investigate unexplained laws of Nature and the powers latent in man.

"The significance of these objectives... should be clear. The first objective implicitly rejects the 'irrational bigotry' and 'sectarianism' of traditional Christianity as perceived by spiritualists and theosophists... It is not immediately obvious from the objectives themselves that, for theosophists, 'science' meant the occult sciences and philosophy the *occulta philosophia*, that the laws of nature were of an occult or psychic nature, and that comparative religion was expected to unveil a 'primordial tradition' ultimately modelled on a Hermeticist *philosophia perennis*".[32]

A prominent component of Mrs Blavatsky's writings was the emancipation of women, which involved an attack on the 'male' God of Judaism, of Christianity and of Islam. She urged people to return to the mother-goddess of Hinduism and to the practice of feminine virtues. This continued under the guidance of Annie Besant, who was in the vanguard of the feminist movement. Wicca and 'women's spirituality' carry on this struggle against 'patriarchal' Christianity today.

Marilyn Ferguson devoted a chapter of *The Aquarian Conspiracy* to the precursors of the Age of Aquarius, those who had woven the threads of a transforming vision based on the expansion of consciousness and the experience of self-transcendence. Two of those she mentioned were the American psychologist William James and the Swiss psychiatrist Carl Gustav Jung. James defined religion as experience, not dogma, and he taught that human beings

---

[32]W.J. Hanegraaff, *op. cit.*, p. 448f. The objectives are quoted from the final (1896) version, earlier versions of which stressed the irrationality of 'bigotry' and the urgency of promoting non-sectarian education. Hanegraaff quotes J. Gordon Melton's description of *New Age* religion as rooted in the 'occult-metaphysical' tradition (*ibid.*, p. 455).

can change their mental attitudes in such a way that they are able to become architects of their own destiny. Jung emphasised the transcendent character of consciousness and introduced the idea of the collective unconscious, a kind of store for symbols and memories shared with people from various different ages and cultures. According to Wouter Hanegraaff, both of these men contributed to a 'sacralisation of psychology', something that has become an important element of *New Age* thought and practice. Jung, indeed, "not only psychologised esotericism but he also sacralised psychology, by filling it with the contents of esoteric speculation. The result was a body of theories which enabled people to talk about God while really meaning their own psyche, and about their own psyche while really meaning the divine. If the psyche is 'mind', and God is 'mind' as well, then to discuss one must mean to discuss the other".[33] His response to the accusation that he had 'psychologised' Christianity was that "psychology is the modern myth and only in terms of the current myth can we understand the faith".[34] It is certainly true that Jung's psychology sheds light on many aspects of the Christian faith, particularly on the need to face the reality of evil, but his religious convictions are so different at different stages of his life that one is left with a confused image of God. A central element in his thought is the cult of the sun, where God is the vital energy (libido) within a person.[35] As he himself said, "this comparison is no mere play of words".[36] This is 'the god within' to which Jung refers, the essential divinity he believed to be in every human being. The path to the inner universe is through the unconscious. The inner world's correspondence to the outer one is in the *collective* unconscious.

The tendency to interchange psychology and spirituality was firmly embedded in the Human Potential Movement as it

[33]W.J. Hanegraaff, *op. cit.,* p. 513.

[34]Thomas M. King s.j., "Jung and Catholic Spirituality", in *America,* 3 April 1999, p. 14. The author points out that New Age devotees "quote passages dealing with the I Ching, astrology and Zen, while Catholics quote passages dealing with Christian mystics, the liturgy and the psychological value of the sacrament of reconciliation" (p. 12). He also lists Catholic personalities and spiritual institutions clearly inspired and guided by Jung's psychology.

[35]Cf. W.J. Hanegraaff, *op. cit.,* p. 501f.

[36]Carl Gustav Jung, *Wandlungen und Symbole der Libido,* quoted in Hanegraaff, *op. cit.,* p. 503.

developed towards the end of the 1960s at the Esalen Institute in California. Transpersonal psychology, strongly influenced by Eastern religions and by Jung, offers a contemplative journey where science meets mysticism. The stress laid on bodiliness, the search for ways of expanding consciousness and the cultivation of the myths of the collective unconscious were all encouragements to search for 'the God within' oneself. To realise one's potential, one had to go beyond one's *ego* in order to become the god that one is, deep down. This could be done by choosing the appropriate therapy - meditation, parapsychological experiences, the use of hallucinogenic drugs. These were all ways of achieving 'peak experiences', 'mystical' experiences of fusion with God and with the cosmos.

The symbol of Aquarius was borrowed from astrological mythology, but later came to signify the desire for a radically new world. The two centres which were the initial power-houses of the *New Age*, and to a certain extent still are, were the Garden community at Findhorn in North-East Scotland, and the Centre for the development of human potential at Esalen in Big Sur, California, in the United States of America. What feeds *New Age* consistently is a growing global consciousness and increasing awareness of a looming ecological crisis.

2.3.3. Central themes of the New Age

New Age is not, properly speaking, a religion, but it is interested in what is called 'divine'. The essence of *New Age* is the loose association of the various activities, ideas and people who might validly attract the term. So there is no single articulation of anything like the doctrines of mainstream religions. Despite this, and despite the immense variety within *New Age*, there are some common points:

- the cosmos is seen as an organic whole

- it is animated by an Energy, which is also identified as the divine Soul or Spirit

- much credence is given to the mediation of various spiritual entities - humans are capable of ascending to invisible higher spheres, and of controlling their own lives beyond death

- there is held to be a 'perennial knowledge' which pre-dates and is superior to all religions and cultures
- people follow enlightened masters...

2.3.4. What does New Age say about...

2.3.4.1. ...the human person?

New Age involves a fundamental belief in the perfectibility of the human person by means of a wide variety of techniques and therapies (as opposed to the Christian view of co-operation with divine grace). There is a general accord with Nietzsche's idea that Christianity has prevented the full manifestation of genuine humanity. Perfection, in this context, means achieving self-fulfilment, according to an order of values which we ourselves create and which we achieve by our own strength: hence one can speak of a self-creating self. On this view, there is more difference between humans as they now are and as they will be when they have fully realised their potential, than there is between humans and anthropoids.

It is useful to distinguish between *esotericism*, a search for knowledge, and *magic*, or the occult: the latter is a means of obtaining power. Some groups are both esoteric and occult. At the centre of occultism is a will to power based on the dream of becoming divine.

Mind-expanding techniques are meant to reveal to people their divine power; by using this power, people prepare the way for the Age of Enlightenment. This exaltation of humanity overturns the correct relationship between Creator and creature, and one of its extreme forms is Satanism. Satan becomes the symbol of a rebellion against conventions and rules, a symbol that often takes aggressive, selfish and violent forms. Some evangelical groups have expressed concern at the subliminal presence of what they claim is Satanic symbolism in some varieties of rock music, which have a powerful influence on young people. This is all far removed from the message of peace and harmony which is to be found in the New Testament; it is often one of the consequences of the exaltation of humanity when that involves the negation of a transcendent God.

But it is not only something which affects young people; the basic themes of esoteric culture are also present in the realms of politics, education and legislation.[37] *It is especially the case with ecology.* Deep ecology's emphasis on bio-centrism denies the anthropological vision of the Bible, in which human beings are at the centre of the world, since they are considered to be qualitatively superior to other natural forms. It is very prominent in legislation and education today, despite the fact that it underrates humanity in this way... The same esoteric cultural matrix can be found in the ideological theory underlying population control policies and experiments in genetic engineering, which seem to express a dream human beings have of creating themselves afresh. How do people hope to do this? By deciphering the genetic code, altering the natural rules of sexuality, defying the limits of death.

In what might be termed a classical *New Age* account, people are born with a divine spark, in a sense which is reminiscent of ancient gnosticism; this links them into the unity of the Whole. So they are seen as essentially divine, although they participate in this cosmic divinity at different levels of consciousness. We are co-creators, and we create our own reality. Many *New Age* authors maintain that we choose the circumstances of our lives (even our own illness and health), in a vision where every individual is considered the creative source of the universe. But we need to make a journey in order fully to understand where we fit into the unity of the cosmos. The journey is psychotherapy, and the recognition of universal consciousness is salvation. There is no sin; there is only imperfect knowledge. The identity of every human being is diluted in the universal being and in the process of successive incarnations. People are subject to the determining influences of the stars, but can be opened to the divinity which lives within them, in their continual search (by means of appropriate techniques) for an ever greater harmony between the self and divine cosmic energy. There is no need for Revelation or Salvation which would come to people from outside themselves, but simply a need to experience the salvation

[37]On this point cf. Michel Schooyans, *L'Évangile face au désordre mondial,* with a preface by Cardinal Joseph Ratzinger, Paris (Fayard) 1997.

hidden within themselves (self-salvation), by mastering psycho-physical techniques which lead to definitive enlightenment.

Some stages on the way to self-redemption are *preparatory* (meditation, body harmony, releasing self-healing energies). They are the starting-point for processes of spiritualisation, perfection and enlightenment which help people to acquire further self-control and psychic concentration on 'transformation' of the individual self into 'cosmic consciousness'. The destiny of the human person is a series of successive reincarnations of the soul in different bodies. This is understood not as the cycle of *samsara*, in the sense of purification as punishment, but as a gradual ascent towards the perfect development of one's potential.

Psychology is used to explain mind expansion as 'mystical' experiences. Yoga, zen, transcendental meditation and tantric exercises lead to an experience of self-fulfilment or enlightenment. Peak-experiences (reliving one's birth, travelling to the gates of death, biofeedback, dance and even drugs - anything which can provoke an altered state of consciousness) are believed to lead to unity and enlightenment. Since there is only one Mind, some people can be *channels* for higher beings. Every part of this single universal being has contact with every other part. The classic approach in *New Age* is transpersonal psychology, whose main concepts are the Universal Mind, the Higher Self, the collective and personal unconscious and the individual ego. The Higher Self is our real identity, a bridge between God as divine Mind and humanity. Spiritual development is contact with the Higher Self, which overcomes all forms of dualism between subject and object, life and death, psyche and soma, the self and the fragmentary aspects of the self. Our limited personality is like a shadow or a dream created by the real self. The Higher Self contains the memories of earlier (re-)incarnations.

2.3.4.2. ...God?

New Age has a marked preference for Eastern or pre-Christian religions, which are reckoned to be uncontaminated by Judaeo-Christian distorsions. Hence great respect is given to ancient agricultural rites and to fertility cults. 'Gaia', Mother Earth, is offered as an alternative to God the Father, whose image is seen to be linked to a patriarchal conception of male domination of women. There is talk of God, but it is not a personal God; the God of which *New Age* speaks is neither personal nor transcendent. Nor is it the Creator and sustainer of the universe, but an 'impersonal energy' immanent in the world, with which it forms a 'cosmic unity': 'All is one'. This unity is monistic, pantheistic or, more precisely, panentheistic. God is the 'life-principle', the 'spirit or soul of the world', the sum total of consciousness existing in the world. In a sense, everything is God. God's presence is clearest in the spiritual aspects of reality, so every mind/spirit is, in some sense, God.

When it is consciously received by men and women, 'divine energy' is often described as 'Christic energy'. There is also talk of Christ, but this does not mean Jesus of Nazareth. 'Christ' is a title applied to someone who has arrived at a state of consciousness where he or she perceives him or herself to be divine and can thus claim to be a 'universal Master'. Jesus of Nazareth was not *the* Christ, but simply one among many historical figures in whom this 'Christic' nature is revealed, as is the case with Buddha and others. Every historical realisation of the *Christ* shows clearly that all human beings are heavenly and divine, and leads them towards this realisation.

The innermost and most personal ('psychic') level on which this 'divine cosmic energy' is 'heard' by human beings is also called 'Holy Spirit'.

2.3.4.3. ...the world?

The move from a mechanistic model of classical physics to the 'holistic' one of modern atomic and sub-atomic physics, based on the concept of matter as waves or energy rather than particles, is central to much *New Age* thinking. The universe is an ocean of energy, which is a single whole or a network of links. The energy animating the single organism which is the universe is 'spirit'. There is no alterity between God and the world. The world itself is divine and it undergoes an evolutionary process which leads from inert matter to 'higher and perfect consciousness'. The world is uncreated, eternal and self-sufficient The future of the world is based on an inner dynamism which is necessarily positive and leads to the reconciled (divine) unity of all that exists. God and the world, soul and body, intelligence and feeling, heaven and earth are one immense vibration of energy.

James Lovelock's book on the Gaia Hypothesis claims that "the entire range of living matter on earth, from whales to viruses, and from oaks to algae, could be regarded as constituting a single living entity, capable of manipulating the Earth's atmosphere to suit its overall needs and endowed with faculties and powers far beyond those of its constituent parts".[38] To some, the Gaia hypothesis is "a strange synthesis of individualism and collectivism. It all happens as if *New Age*, having plucked people out of fragmentary politics, cannot wait to throw them into the great cauldron of the global mind". The global brain needs institutions with which to rule, in other words, a world government. "To deal with today's problems *New Age* dreams of a spiritual aristocracy in the style of Plato's *Republic*, run by secret societies...".[39] This may be an exaggerated way of stating the case, but there is much evidence that gnostic élitism and global governance coincide on many issues in international politics.

Everything in the universe is interelated; in fact every part is in itself an image of the totality; the whole is in every thing and every thing is in the whole. In the 'great chain of being', all beings are intimately linked and form one family with different grades of evolution. Every human person is a *hologram*, an image of the whole of creation, in which every thing vibrates on its own frequency. Every human being is a neurone in earth's central nervous system, and all individual entities are in a relationship of complementarity with others. In fact, there is an inner complementarity or androgyny in the whole of creation.[40]

One of the recurring themes in *New Age* writings and thought is the 'new paradigm' which contemporary science has opened up. "Science has given us insights into wholes and systems, stress and transformation. We are learning to read tendencies, to recognise the

---

[38]Quoted in the Maranatha Community's *The True and the False New Age. Introductory Ecumenical Notes,* Manchester (Maranatha) 1993, 8.10 - the original page numbering is not specified.
[39]Michel Lacroix, *L'Ideologia della New Age,* Milano (il Saggiatore) 1998, p. 84f.
[40]Cf. the section on David Spangler's ideas in *Actualité des religions* n° 8, septembre 1999, p. 43.

early signs of another, more promising, paradigm. We create alternative scenarios of the future. We communicate about the failures of old systems, forcing new frameworks for problem-solving in every area".[41] Thus far, the 'paradigm shift' is a radical change of perspective, but nothing more. The question is whether thought and real change are commensurate, and how effective in the external world an inner transformation can be proved to be. One is forced to ask, even without expressing a negative judgement, how scientific a thought-process can be when it involves affirmations like this: "War is unthinkable in a society of autonomous people who have discovered the connectedness of all humanity, who are unafraid of alien ideas and alien cultures, who know that all revolutions begin within and that you cannot impose your brand of enlightenment on anyone else".[42] It is illogical to conclude from the fact that something is unthinkable that it cannot happen. Such reasoning is really gnostic, in the sense of giving too much power to knowledge and consciousness. This is not to deny the fundamental and crucial role of developing consciousness in scientific discovery and creative development, but simply to caution against imposing upon external reality what is as yet still only in the mind.

2.4. "Inhabitants of myth rather than history"[43]?: *New Age* and culture

"Basically, the appeal of the *New Age* has to do with the culturally stimulated interest in the self, its value, capacities and problems. Whereas traditionalised religiosity, with its hierarchical organisation, is well-suited for the community, detraditionalised spirituality is well-suited for the individual. The *New Age* is 'of' the self in that it facilitates celebration of what it is to be and to become; and 'for' the self in that by differing from much of the mainstream, it is positioned to handle identity problems generated by conventional forms of life".[44]

---

[41] M. Ferguson, *op. cit.,* p. 407.

[42] *Ibid.,* p. 411.

[43] "To be an American... is precisely to *imagine* a destiny rather than inherit one. We have always been inhabitants of myth rather than history": Leslie Fiedler, quoted in M. Ferguson, *op. cit.,* p. 142.

[44] Cf. P. Heelas, *op. cit.,* p. 173f.

The rejection of tradition in the form of patriarchal, hierarchical social or ecclesial organisation implies the search for an alternative form of society, one that is clearly inspired by the modern notion of the self. Many *New Age* writings argue that one can do nothing (directly) to change the world, but everything to change oneself; changing individual consciousness is understood to be the (indirect) way to change the world. The most important instrument for social change is personal example. Worldwide recognition of these personal examples will steadily lead to the transformation of the collective mind and such a transformation will be the major achievement of our time. This is clearly part of the holistic paradigm, and a re-statement of the classical philosophical question of the one and the many. It is also linked to Jung's espousal of the theory of correspondence and his rejection of causality. Individuals are fragmentary representations of the planetary hologram; by looking within one not only *knows* the universe, but also *changes* it. But the more one looks within, the smaller the political arena becomes. Does this really fit in with the rhetoric of democratic participation in a new planetary order, or is it an unconscious and subtle disempowerment of people, which could leave them open to manipulation? Does the current preoccupation with planetary problems (ecological issues, depletion of resources, over-population, the economic gap between north and south, the huge nuclear arsenal and political instability) enable or disable engagement in other, equally real, political and social questions? The old adage that 'charity begins at home' can give a healthy balance to one's approach to these issues. Some observers of *New Age* detect a sinister authoritarianism behind apparent indifference to politics. David Spangler himself points out that one of the shadows of the *New Age* is "a subtle surrender to powerlessness and irresponsibility in the name of waiting for the *New Age* to come rather than being an active creator of wholeness in one's own life".[45]

Even though it would hardly be correct to suggest that quietism is universal in *New Age* attitudes, one of the chief criticisms of the *New Age* Movement is that its privatistic quest for self-fulfilment

[45] David Spangler, *The New Age,* Issaquah (Mornington Press) 1988, p. 14.

may actually work against the possibility of a sound religious culture. Three points bring this into focus:

- it is questionable whether *New Age* demonstrates the *intellectual cogency* to provide a complete picture of the cosmos in a world view which claims to integrate nature and spiritual reality. The Western universe is seen as a divided one based on monotheism, transcendence, alterity and separateness. A fundamental dualism is detected in such divisions as those between real and ideal, relative and absolute, finite and infinite, human and divine, sacred and profane, past and present, all redolent of Hegel's 'unhappy consciousness'. This is portrayed as something tragic. The response from *New Age* is unity through fusion: it claims to reconcile soul and body, female and male, spirit and matter, human and divine, earth and cosmos, transcendent and immanent, religion and science, differences between religions, Yin and Yang. There is, thus, no more alterity; what is left in human terms is transpersonality. The *New Age* world is unproblematic: there is nothing left to achieve. But the metaphysical question of the one and the many remains unanswered, perhaps even unasked, in that there is a great deal of regret at the effects of disunity and division, but the response is a description of how things would appear in another vision.

- *New Age* imports Eastern religious practices piecemeal and *re-interprets them to suit Westerners;* this involves a rejection of the language of sin and salvation, replacing it with the morally neutral language of addiction and recovery. References to extra-European influences are sometimes merely a 'pseudo-Orientalisation' of Western culture. Furthermore, it is hardly a genuine dialogue; in a context where Graeco-Roman and Judaeo-Christian influences are suspect, oriental influences are used precisely because they are alternatives to Western culture. Traditional science and medicine are felt to be inferior to holistic approaches, as are patriarchal and particular structures in politics and religion. All of these will be obstacles to the coming of the Age of Aquarius; once again, it is clear that what is implied when people opt for *New Age* alternatives is a complete break with the tradition that formed them. Is this as mature and liberated as it is often thought or presumed to be?

- Authentic religious traditions encourage discipline with the eventual goal of acquiring *wisdom, equanimity and compassion. New Age* echoes society's deep, ineradicable yearning for an integral religious culture, and for something more generic and enlightened than what politicians generally offer, but it is not clear whether the benefits of a vision based on the ever-expanding self are for individuals or for societies. *New Age* training courses (what used to be known as 'Erhard seminar trainings' [EST] etc.) marry counter-cultural values with the mainstream need to succeed, inner satisfaction with outer success; Findhorn's 'Spirit of Business' retreat transforms the experience of work while increasing productivity; some *New Age* devotees are involved not only to become more authentic and spontaneous, but also in order to become more prosperous (through magic etc.). "What makes things even more appealing to the enterprise-minded businessperson is that *New Age* trainings also resonate with somewhat more humanistic ideas abroad in the world of business. The ideas have to do with the workplace as a 'learning environment', 'bringing life back to work', 'humanising work', 'fulfilling the manager', 'people come first' or 'unlocking potential'. Presented by *New Age* trainers, they are likely to appeal to those businesspeople who have already been involved with more (secular) humanistic trainings and who want to take things further: at one and the same time for the sake of personal growth, happiness and enthusiasm, as well as for commercial productivity".[46] So it is clear that people involved do seek wisdom and equanimity for their own benefit, but how much do the activities in which they are involved enable them to work for the common good? Apart from the question of motivation, all of these phenomena need to be judged by their fruits, and the question to ask is whether they promote *self* or *solidarity*, not only with whales, trees or like-minded people, but with the whole of creation - including the whole of humanity. The most pernicious consequences of any philosophy of egoism which is embraced by institutions or by large numbers of people are identified by Cardinal Joseph Ratzinger as a set of "strategies to reduce the number of those who will eat at humanity's

[46] P. Heelas, *op. cit.*, p. 168.

table".[47] This is a key standard by which to evaluate the impact of any philosophy or theory. Christianity always seeks to measure human endeavours by their openness to the Creator and to all other creatures, a respect based firmly on love.

2.5. Why has *New Age* grown so rapidly and spread so effectively?

Whatever questions and criticisms it may attract, *New Age* is an attempt by people who experience the world as harsh and heartless to bring warmth to that world. As a reaction to modernity, it operates more often than not on the level of feelings, instincts and emotions. Anxiety about an apocalyptic future of economic instability, political uncertainty and climatic change plays a large part in causing people to look for an alternative, resolutely optimistic relationship to the cosmos. There is a search for wholeness and happiness, often on an explicitly spiritual level. But it is significant that *New Age* has enjoyed enormous success in an era which can be characterised by the almost universal exaltation of *diversity*. Western culture has taken a step beyond tolerance - in the sense of grudging acceptance or putting up with the idiosyncrasies of a person or a minority group - to a conscious erosion of respect for normality. Normality is presented as a morally loaded concept, linked necessarily with absolute norms. For a growing number of people, absolute beliefs or norms indicate nothing but an inability to tolerate other people's views and convictions. In this atmosphere alternative life-styles and theories have really taken off: it is not only acceptable but positively good to be diverse.[48]

It is essential to bear in mind that people are involved with *New Age* in very different ways and on many levels. In most cases it is not really a question of 'belonging' to a group or movement; nor is there much conscious awareness of the principles on which *New Age* is built. It seems that, for the most part, people are attracted to

[47]See the Preface to Michel Schooyans, *L'Évangile face au désordre mondial, op. cit.* This quotation is translated from the Italian, *Il nuovo disordine mondiale,* Cinisello Balsamo (San Paolo) 2000, p. 6.

[48]Cf. *Our Creative Diversity. Report of the World Commission on Culture and Development,* Paris (UNESCO) 1995, which illustrates the importance given to celebrating and promoting diversity.

particular therapies or practices, without going into their background, and others are simply occasional consumers of products which are labelled '*New Age*'. People who use aromatherapy or listen to '*New Age*' music, for example, are usually interested in the effect they have on their health or well-being; it is only a minority who go further into the subject, and try to understand its theoretical (or 'mystical') significance. This fits perfectly into the patterns of consumption in societies where amusement and leisure play such an important part. The 'movement' has adapted well to the laws of the market, and it is partly because it is such an attractive economic proposition that *New Age* has become so widespread. *New Age* has been seen, in some cultures at least, as the label for a product created by the application of marketing principles to a religious phenomenon.[49] There is always going to be a way of profiting from people's perceived spiritual needs. Like many other things in contemporary economics, *New Age* is a global phenomenon held together and fed with information by the mass media. It is arguable that this global community was created by means of the mass media, and it is quite clear that popular literature and mass communications ensure that the common notions held by 'believers' and sympathisers spread almost everywhere very rapidly. However, there is no way of proving that such a rapid spread of ideas is either by chance or by design, since this is a very loose form of 'community'. Like the cybercommunities created by the Internet, it is a domain where relationships between people can be either very impersonal or interpersonal in only a very selective sense.

New Age has become immensely popular as a loose set of beliefs, therapies and practices, which are often selected and combined at will, irrespective of the incompatibilities and inconsistencies this may imply. But this is obviously to be expected in a world-view self-consciously based on 'right-brain' intuitive thinking. And that is precisely why it is important to discover and recognise the fundamental characteristics of *New Age* ideas. What is offered is

---

[49]Cf. Christoph Bochinger, *"New Age" und moderne Religion: Religionswissenschaftliche Untersuchungen,* Gütersloh (Kaiser) 1994, especially chapter 3.

often described as simply 'spiritual', rather than belonging to any religion, but there are much closer links to particular Eastern religions than many 'consumers' realise. This is obviously important in 'prayer'-groups to which people choose to belong, but it is also a real question for management in a growing number of companies, whose employees are required to practise meditation and adopt mind-expanding techniques as part of their life at work.[50]

It is worth saying a brief word about concerted promotion of *New Age* as an ideology, but this is a very complex issue. Some groups have reacted to *New Age* with sweeping accusations about conspiracies, but the answer would generally be that we are witnessing a spontaneous cultural change whose course is fairly determined by influences beyond human control. However, it is enough to point out that *New Age* shares with a number of internationally influential groups the goal of superseding or transcending particular religions in order to create space for a universal religion which could unite humanity. Closely related to this is a very concerted effort on the part of many institutions to invent a *Global Ethic*, an ethical framework which would reflect the global nature of contemporary culture, economics and politics. Further, the politicisation of ecological questions certainly colours the whole question of the Gaia hypothesis or worship of mother earth.

---

[50]The shortcomings of techniques which are not yet prayer are discussed below in § 3.4, "Christian mysticism and *New Age* mysticism".

3. *NEW AGE* AND CHRISTIAN SPIRITUALITY

3.1. *New Age* as spirituality

New Age is often referred to by those who promote it as a 'new spirituality'. It seems ironic to call it 'new' when so many of its ideas have been taken from ancient religions and cultures. But what really is new is that *New Age* is a conscious search for an alternative to Western culture and its Judaeo-Christian religious roots. 'Spirituality' in this way refers to the inner experience of harmony and unity with the whole of reality, which heals each human person's feelings of imperfection and finiteness. People discover their profound connectedness with the sacred universal force or energy which is the nucleus of all life. When they have made this discovery, men and women can set out on a path to perfection, which will enable them to sort out their personal lives and their relationship to the world, and to take their place in the universal process of becoming and in the New Genesis of a world in constant evolution. The result is a *cosmic mysticism*[51] based on people's awareness of a universe burgeoning with dynamic energies. Thus cosmic energy, vibration, light, God, love - even the supreme Self - all refer to one and the same reality, the primal source present in every being.

This spirituality consists of two distinct elements, one metaphysical, the other psychological. The *metaphysical* component comes from *New Age*'s esoteric and theosophical roots, and is basically a new form of gnosis. Access to the divine is by knowledge of hidden mysteries, in each individual's search for "the real behind what is only apparent, the origin beyond time, the transcendent beyond what is merely fleeting, the primordial tradition behind merely ephemeral tradition, the other behind the self, the cosmic divinity beyond the incarnate individual". Esoteric spirituality "is an investigation of Being beyond the separateness of beings, a sort of nostalgia for lost unity".[52]

---

[51]Cf. Carlo Maccari, "La 'mistica cosmica' del *New Age*", in *Religioni e Sette nel Mondo* 1996/2.
[52]Jean Vernette, "L'avventura spirituale dei figli dell'Acquario", in *Religioni e Sette nel Mondo* 1996/2, p. 42f.

"Here one can see the gnostic matrix of esoteric spirituality. It is evident when the children of Aquarius search for the Transcendent Unity of religions. They tend to pick out of the historical religions only the esoteric nucleus, whose guardians they claim to be. They somehow deny history and will not accept that spirituality can be rooted in time or in any institution. Jesus of Nazareth is not God, but one of the many historical manifestations of the cosmic and universal Christ".[53]

The *psychological* component of this kind of spirituality comes from the encounter between esoteric culture and psychology (cf. 2.3.2). *New Age* thus becomes an experience of personal psycho-spiritual transformation, seen as analogous to religious experience. For some people this transformation takes the form of a deep mystical experience, after a personal crisis or a lengthy spiritual search. For others it comes from the use of meditation or some sort of therapy, or from paranormal experiences which alter states of consciousness and provide insight into the unity of reality.[54]

3.2. Spiritual narcissism?

Several authors see *New Age* spirituality as a kind of spiritual narcissism or pseudo-mysticism. It is interesting to note that this criticism was put forward even by an important exponent of *New Age*, David Spangler, who, in his later works, distanced himself from the more esoteric aspects of this current of thought.

He wrote that, in the more popular forms of *New Age*, "individuals and groups are living out their own fantasies of adventure and power, usually of an occult or millenarian form... The principal characteristic of this level is attachment to a private world of ego-fulfilment and a consequent (though not always apparent) withdrawal from the world. On this level, the *New Age* has become populated with strange and exotic beings, masters, adepts, extraterrestrials; it is a place of psychic powers and occult mysteries, of conspiracies and hidden teachings".[55]

---

[53]J. Vernette, *loc. cit.*

[54]Cf. J. Gordon Melton, *New Age Encyclopedia,* Detroit (Gale Research) 1990, pp. xiii-xiv.

[55]David Spangler, *The Rebirth of the Sacred,* London (Gateway Books) 1984, p. 78f.

In a later work, David Spangler lists what he sees as the negative elements or 'shadows' of the *New Age*: "alienation from the past in the name of the future; attachment to novelty for its own sake...; indiscriminateness and lack of discernment in the name of wholeness and communion, hence the failure to understand or respect the role of boundaries...; confusion of psychic phenomena with wisdom, of channeling with spirituality, of the *New Age* perspective with ultimate truth".[56] But, in the end, Spangler is convinced that selfish, irrational narcissism is limited to just a few new-agers. The positive aspects he stresses are the function of *New Age* as an image of change and as an incarnation of the sacred, a movement in which most people are "very serious seekers after truth", working in the interest of life and inner growth.

The commercial aspect of many products and therapies which bear the *New Age* label is brought out by David Toolan, an American Jesuit who spent several years in the *New Age* milieu. He observes that new-agers have discovered the inner life and are fascinated by the prospect of being responsible for the world, but that they are also easily overcome by a tendency to individualism and to viewing everything as an object of consumption. In this sense, while it is not Christian, *New Age* spirituality is not Buddhist either, inasmuch as it does not involve self-denial. The dream of mystical union seems to lead, in practice, to a merely virtual union, which, in the end, leaves people more alone and unsatisfied.

3.3. The Cosmic Christ

In the early days of Christianity, believers in Jesus Christ were forced to face up to the gnostic religions. They did not ignore them, but took the challenge positively and applied the terms used of cosmic deities to Christ himself. The clearest example of this is in the famous hymn to Christ in Saint Paul's letter to the Christians at Colossae:

"He is the image of the unseen God and the first-born of all creation,
for in him were created all things in heaven and on earth:
everything visible and everything invisible,

---

[56] David Spangler, *The New Age, op. cit.*, p. 13f.

Thrones, Dominations, Sovereignties, Powers -
all things were created through him and for him.
Before anything was created, he existed, and he holds all things in unity.
Now the Church is his body, he is its head.
As he is the Beginning, he was first to be born from the dead,
so that he should be first in every way;
because God wanted all perfection to be found in him
and all things to be reconciled through him and for him,
everything in heaven and everything on earth,
when he made peace by his death on the cross" (*Col* 1:15-20).

For these early Christians, there was no new cosmic age to come; what they were celebrating with this hymn was the Fulfilment of all things which had begun in Christ. "Time is indeed fulfilled by the very fact that God, in the Incarnation, came down into human history. Eternity entered into time: what 'fulfilment' could be greater than this? What other 'fulfilment' would be possible?"[57] Gnostic belief in cosmic powers and some obscure kind of destiny withdraws the possibility of a relationship to a personal God revealed in Christ. For Christians, the real cosmic Christ is the one who is present actively in the various members of his body, which is the Church. They do not look to impersonal cosmic powers, but to the loving care of a *personal* God; for them cosmic bio-centrism has to be transposed into a set of *social* relationships (in the Church); and they are not locked into a cyclical pattern of cosmic events, but focus on the *historical* Jesus, in particular on his crucifixion and resurrection. We find in the Letter to the Colossians and in the New Testament a doctrine of God different from that implicit in *New Age* thought: the Christian conception of God is one of a Trinity of Persons who has created the human race out of a desire to share the communion of Trinitarian life with creaturely persons. Properly understood, this means that authentic spirituality is not so much *our* search for God but *God's* search for us.

Another, completely different, view of the cosmic significance of Christ has become current in *New Age* circles. "The Cosmic Christ is

[57] John Paul II, Apostolic Letter *Tertio Millennio Adveniente* (10 November 1994), 9.

the *divine* pattern that connects in the person of Jesus Christ (but by no means is limited to that person). The divine pattern of connectivity *was made flesh and set up its tent among us* (*John* 1:14)... The Cosmic Christ... leads a new exodus from the bondage and pessimistic views of a Newtonian, mechanistic universe so ripe with competition, winners and losers, dualisms, anthropocentrism, and the boredom that comes when our exciting universe is pictured as a machine bereft of mystery and mysticism. The Cosmic Christ is local and historical, indeed intimate to human history. The Cosmic Christ might be living next door or even inside one's deepest and truest self".[58] Although this statement may not satisfy everyone involved in *New Age*, it does catch the tone very well, and it shows with absolute clarity where the differences between these two views of Christ lie. For *New Age* the Cosmic Christ is seen as a pattern which can be repeated in many people, places and times; it is the bearer of an enormous paradigm shift; it is ultimately a potential within us.

According to Christian belief, Jesus Christ is not a pattern, but a divine person whose human-divine figure reveals the mystery of the Father's love for every person throughout history (*Jn* 3:16); he lives in us because he shares his life with us, but it is neither imposed nor automatic. All men and women are invited to share his life, to live 'in Christ'.

3.4. Christian mysticism and *New Age* mysticism

For Christians, the spiritual life is a relationship with God which gradually through his grace becomes deeper, and in the process also sheds light on our relationship with our fellow men and women, and with the universe. Spirituality in *New Age* terms means experiencing states of consciousness dominated by a sense of harmony and fusion with the Whole. So "mysticism" refers not to meeting the transcendent God in the fullness of love, but to the experience engendered by turning in on oneself, an exhilarating sense of being at one with the universe, a sense of letting one's individuality sink into the great ocean of Being.[59]

---

[58]Matthew Fox, *The Coming of the Cosmic Christ. The Healing of Mother Earth and the Birth of a Global Renaissance,* San Francisco (Harper & Row) 1988, p. 135.

[59]Cf. the document issued by the Argentine Bishops' Conference Committee for Culture: *Frente a una Nueva Era. Desafío a la pastoral en el horizonte de la Nueva Evangelización,* 1993.

This fundamental distinction is evident at all levels of comparison between Christian mysticism and *New Age* mysticism. The *New Age* way of purification is based on awareness of unease or alienation, which is to be overcome by immersion into the Whole. In order to be converted, a person needs to make use of techniques which lead to the experience of illumination. This transforms a person's consciousness and opens him or her to contact with the divinity, which is understood as the deepest essence of reality.

The techniques and methods offered in this immanentist religious system, which has no concept of God as person, proceed 'from below'. Although they involve a descent into the depths of one's own heart or soul, they constitute an essentially human enterprise on the part of a person who seeks to rise towards divinity by his or her own efforts. It is often an 'ascent' on the level of consciousness to what is understood to be a liberating awareness of 'the god within'. Not everyone has access to these techniques, whose benefits are restricted to a privileged spiritual 'aristocracy'.

The essential element in Christian faith, however, is God's descent towards his creatures, particularly towards the humblest, those who are weakest and least gifted according to the values of the 'world'. There are spiritual techniques which it is useful to learn, but God is able to by-pass them or do without them. A Christian's "method of getting closer to God is not based on any *technique* in the strict sense of the word. That would contradict the spirit of childhood called for by the Gospel. The heart of genuine Christian mysticism is not technique: it is always a gift of God; and the one who benefits from it knows himself to be unworthy".[60]

For Christians, conversion is turning back to the Father, through the Son, in docility to the power of the Holy Spirit. The more people progress in their relationship with God - which is always and in every way a free gift - the more acute is the need to be converted from sin, spiritual myopia and self-infatuation, all of which obstruct a trusting self-abandonment to God and openness to other men and women.

All meditation techniques need to be purged of presumption and pretentiousness. Christian prayer is not an exercise in self-

[60]Congregation for the Doctrine of the Faith, *Orationis Formas,* 23.

contemplation, stillness and self-emptying, but a dialogue of love, one which "implies an attitude of conversion, a flight from 'self' to the 'You' of God".[61] It leads to an increasingly complete surrender to God's will, whereby we are invited to a deep, genuine solidarity with our brothers and sisters.[62]

3.5. The 'god within' and 'theosis'

Here is a key point of contrast between *New Age* and Christianity. So much *New Age* literature is shot through with the conviction that there is no divine being 'out there', or in any real way distinct from the rest of reality. From Jung's time onwards there has been a stream of people professing belief in 'the god within'. Our problem, in a *New Age* perspective, is our inability to recognise our own divinity, an inability which can be overcome with the help of guidance and the use of a whole variety of techniques for unlocking our hidden (divine) potential. The fundamental idea is that 'God' is deep within ourselves. We are gods, and we discover the unlimited power within us by peeling off layers of inauthenticity.[63] The more this potential is recognised, the more it is realised, and in this sense the *New Age* has its own idea of *theosis*, becoming divine or, more precisely, recognising and accepting that we are divine. We are said by some to be living in "an age in which our understanding of God has to be interiorised: from the Almighty God out there to God the dynamic, creative power within the very centre of all being: God as Spirit".[64]

In the Preface to Book V of *Adversus Haereses,* Saint Irenaeus refers to "Jesus Christ, who did, through His transcendent love, become what we are, that He might bring us to be even what He is Himself". Here *theosis*, the Christian understanding of divinisation, comes about not through our own efforts alone, but with the assistance of God's grace working in and through us. It inevitably

---

[61] *Ibid.,* 3. See the sections on meditation and contemplative prayer in the *Catechism of the Catholic Church,* §§. 2705-2719.

[62] Cf. Congregation for the Doctrine of the Faith, *Orationis Formas,* 13.

[63] Cf. Brendan Pelphrey, "I said, You are Gods. Orthodox Christian *Theosis* and Deification in the New Religious Movements" in *Spirituality East and West,* Easter 2000 (No. 13).

[64] Adrian Smith, *God and the Aquarian Age. The new era of the Kingdom,* Great Wakering (McCrimmons) 1990, p. 49.

involves an initial awareness of incompleteness and even sinfulness, in no way an exaltation of the self. Furthermore, it unfolds as an introduction into the life of the Trinity, a perfect case of distinction at the heart of unity; it is synergy rather than fusion. This all comes about as the result of a personal encounter, an offer of a new kind of life. Life in Christ is not something so personal and private that it is restricted to the realm of consciousness. Nor is it merely a new level of awareness. It involves being transformed in our soul and in our body by participation in the sacramental life of the Church.

4. *NEW AGE* AND CHRISTIAN FAITH IN CONTRAST

It is difficult to separate the individual elements of *New Age* religiosity - innocent though they may appear - from the overarching framework which permeates the whole thought-world on the *New Age* movement. The gnostic nature of this movement calls us to judge it in its entirety. From the point of view of Christian faith, it is not possible to isolate some elements of *New Age* religiosity as acceptable to Christians, while rejecting others. Since the *New Age* movement makes much of a communication with nature, of cosmic knowledge of a universal good - thereby negating the revealed contents of Christian faith - it cannot be viewed as positive or innocuous. In a cultural environment, marked by religious relativism, it is necessary to signal a warning against the attempt to place *New Age* religiosity on the same level as Christian faith, making the difference between faith and belief seem relative, thus creating greater confusion for the unwary. In this regard, it is useful to remember the exhortation of St Paul "to instruct certain people not to teach false doctrine or to concern themselves with myths and endless genealogies, which promote speculations rather than the plan of God that is to be received by faith" (*1 Tim* 1:3-4). Some practices are incorrectly labeled as *New Age* simply as a marketing strategy to make them sell better, but are not truly associated with its worldview. This only adds to the confusion. It is therefore necessary to accurately identify those elements which belong to the *New Age* movement, and which cannot be accepted by those who are faithful to Christ and his Church.

The following questions may be the easiest key to evaluating some of the central elements of *New Age* thought and practice from a Christian standpoint. '*New Age*' refers to the ideas which circulate about God, the human being and the world, the people with whom Christians may have conversations on religious matters, the publicity material for meditation groups, therapies and the like, explicit statements on religion and so on. Some of these questions applied to people and ideas not explicitly labelled *New*

Age would reveal further unnamed or unacknowledged links with the whole *New Age* atmosphere.

• Is God a being with whom we have a relationship or something to be used or a force to be harnessed?

The *New Age* concept of God is rather diffuse, whereas the Christian concept is a very clear one. The *New Age* god is an impersonal energy, really a particular extension or component of the cosmos; god in this sense is the life-force or soul of the world. Divinity is to be found in every being, in a gradation "from the lowest crystal of the mineral world up to and beyond the Galactic God himself, about Whom we can say nothing at all. This is not a man but a Great Consciousness".[65] In some 'classic' *New Age* writings, it is clear that human beings are meant to think of themselves as gods: this is more fully developed in some people than in others. God is no longer to be sought beyond the world, but deep within myself.[66] Even when 'God' is something outside myself, it is there to be manipulated.

This is very different from the Christian understanding of God as the maker of heaven and earth and the source of all personal life. God is in himself personal, the Father, Son and Holy Spirit, who created the universe in order to share the communion of his life with creaturely persons. "God, who 'dwells in unapprochable light', wants to communicate his own divine life to the men he freely created, in order to adopt them as his sons in his only-begotten Son. By revealing himself God wishes to make them capable of responding to him, and of knowing him, and of loving him far beyond their own natural capacity".[67] God is not identified with the Life-principle understood as the 'Spirit' or 'basic energy' of the cosmos, but is that love which is absolutely different from the world, and yet creatively present in everything, and leading human beings to salvation.

---

[65]Cf. Benjamin Creme, *The Reappearance of Christ and the Masters of Wisdom,* London (Tara Press) 1979, p. 116.

[66]Cf. Jean Vernette, *Le New Age,* Paris (P.U.F.) 1992 (Collection Encyclopédique *Que sais-je?*), p. 14.

[67]*Catechism of the Catholic Church,* 52.

• Is there just one Jesus Christ, or are there thousands of Christs?

Jesus Christ is often presented in *New Age* literature as one among many wise men, or initiates, or avatars, whereas in Christian tradition He is the Son of God. Here are some common points in *New Age* approaches:

- the personal and individual historical Jesus is distinct from the eternal, impersonal universal Christ;

- Jesus is not considered to be the only Christ;

- the death of Jesus on the cross is either denied or re-interpreted to exclude the idea that He, as Christ, could have suffered;

- extra-biblical documents (like the neo-gnostic gospels) are considered authentic sources for the knowledge of aspects of the life of Jesus which are not to be found in the canon of Scripture. Other revelations about Jesus, made available by entities, spirit guides and ascended masters, or even through the *Akasha Chronicles,* are basic for *New Age* christology;

- a kind of esoteric exegesis is applied to biblical texts to purify Christianity of the formal religion which inhibits access to its esoteric essence.[68]

In the Christian Tradition Jesus Christ is the Jesus of Nazareth about which the gospels speak, the son of Mary and the only Son of God, true man and true God, the full revelation of divine truth, unique Saviour of the world: "for our sake he was crucified under Pontius Pilate; he suffered, died and was buried. On the third day he rose again in fulfilment of the Scriptures; he ascended into heaven and is seated at the right hand of the Father".[69]

• The human being: is there one universal being or are there many individuals?

"The point of *New Age* techniques is to reproduce mystical states at will, as if it were a matter of laboratory material. Rebirth, biofeedback, sensory isolation, holotropic breathing, hypnosis, mantras, fasting, sleep deprivation and transcendental meditation are attempts to control these states and to experience them

[68]Cf. Alessandro Olivieri Pennesi, *Il Cristo del New Age. Indagine Critica,* Vatican City (Libreria Editrice Vaticana) 1999, especially pages 13-34. The list of common points is on p. 33.
[69]The Nicene Creed.

continuously".[70] These practices all create an atmosphere of psychic weakness (and vulnerability). When the object of the exercise is that we should re-invent our selves, there is a real question of who 'I' am. 'God within us' and holistic union with the whole cosmos underline this question. Isolated individual personalities would be pathological in terms of *New Age* (in particular transpersonal psychology). But "the real danger is the holistic paradigm. *New Age* is thinking based on totalitarian unity and that is why it is a danger...".[71] More moderately: "We are authentic when we 'take charge of' ourselves, when our choice and reactions flow spontaneously from our deepest needs, when our behaviour and expressed feelings reflect our personal wholeness".[72] The Human Potential Movement is the clearest example of the conviction that humans are divine, or contain a divine spark within themselves.

The Christian approach grows out of the Scriptural teachings about human nature; men and women are created in God's image and likeness (Gen 1:27) and God takes great consideration of them, much to the relieved surprise of the Psalmist (cf. Ps 8). The human person is a mystery fully revealed only in Jesus Christ (cf. GS 22), and in fact becomes authentically human properly in his relationship with Christ through the gift of the Spirit.[73] *This is far from the caricature of anthropocentrism ascribed to Christianity and rejected by many New Age authors and practitioners.*

• Do we save ourselves or is salvation a free gift from God?

The key is to discover by what or by whom we believe we are saved. Do we save ourselves by our own actions, as is often the case in *New Age* explanations, or are we saved by God's love? Key words are *self-fulfilment* and *self-realisation, self-redemption. New Age* is essentially Pelagian in its understanding of human nature.[74]

For Christians, salvation depends on a participation in the passion,

---

[70]Michel Lacroix, *L'Ideologia della New Age,* Milano (Il Saggiatore) 1998, p. 74.
[71]*Ibid.,* p. 68.
[72]Edwin Schur, *The Awareness Trap. Self-Absorption instead of Social Change,* New York (McGraw Hill) 1977, p. 68.
[73]Cf. *Catechism of the Catholic Church,* §§ 355-383.
[74]Cf. Paul Heelas, *The New Age Movement. The Celebration of the Self and the Sacralization of Modernity,* Oxford (Blackwell) 1996, p. 161.

death and resurrection of Christ, and on a direct personal relationship with God rather than on any technique. The human situation, affected as it is by original sin and by personal sin, can only be rectified by God's action: sin is an offense against God, and only God can reconcile us to himself. In the divine plan of salvation, human beings have been saved by Jesus Christ who, as God and man, is the one mediator of redemption. In Christianity salvation is not an experience of self, a meditative and intuitive dwelling within oneself, but much more the forgiveness of sin, being lifted out of profound ambivalences in oneself and the calming of nature by the gift of communion with a loving God. The way to salvation is not found simply in a self-induced transformation of consciousness, but in a liberation from sin and its consequences which then leads us to struggle against sin in ourselves and in the society around us. It necessarily moves us toward loving solidarity with our neighbour in need.

- **Do we invent truth or do we embrace it?**

New Age truth is about good vibrations, cosmic correspondences, harmony and ecstasy, in general pleasant experiences. It is a matter of finding one's own truth in accordance with the feel-good factor. Evaluating religion and ethical questions is obviously relative to one's own feelings and experiences.

Jesus Christ is presented in Christian teaching as "The Way, the Truth and the Life" (Jn 14:6). His followers are asked to open their whole lives to him and to his values, in other words to an objective set of requirements which are part of an objective reality ultimately knowable by all.

- **Prayer and meditation: are we talking to ourselves or to God?**

The tendency to confuse psychology and spirituality makes it hard not to insist that many of the meditation techniques now used are not prayer. They are often a good preparation for prayer, but no more, even if they lead to a more pleasant state of mind or bodily comfort. The experiences involved are genuinely intense, but to remain at this level is to remain alone, not yet in the presence of the other. The achievement of silence can confront us with emptiness, rather than the silence of contemplating the beloved. It is also true that techniques for going deeper into one's own soul are ultimately an appeal to one's own ability to reach the divine, or even to become divine: if they forget God's search for the human heart they are still not Christian prayer. Even when it is seen as a link with the Universal Energy, "such an easy 'relationship' with God, where God's function is seen as supplying all our needs, shows the selfishness at the heart of this *New Age*".[75]

New Age practices are not really prayer, in that they are generally a question of introspection or fusion with cosmic energy, as opposed to the double orientation of Christian prayer, which involves introspection but is essentially also a meeting with God. Far from being a merely human effort, Christian mysticism is essentially a dialogue which "implies an attitude of conversion, a flight from 'self' to the 'you' of God".[76] "The Christian, even when he is alone and prays in secret, he is conscious that he always prays for the good of the Church in union with Christ, in the Holy Spirit and together with all the saints".[77]

• Are we tempted to deny sin or do we accept that there is such a thing?

In *New Age* there is no real concept of sin, but rather one of imperfect knowledge; what is needed is enlightenment, which can be reached through particular psycho-physical techniques. Those who take part in *New Age* activities will not be told what to believe, what to do or what not to do, but: "There are a thousand ways of exploring inner reality. Go where your intelligence and intuition lead you. Trust yourself".[78] Authority has shifted from a theistic location to within the self. The most serious problem perceived in *New Age* thinking is alienation from the whole cosmos, rather than personal failure or sin. The remedy is to become more and more immersed in the whole of being. In some *New Age* writings and practices, it is clear that one life is not enough, so there have to be reincarnations to allow people to realise their full potential.

---

[75] *A Catholic Response to the New Age Phenomenon,* Irish Theological Commission 1994, chapter 3.
[76] Congregation for the Doctrine of the Faith, *Orationis Formas,* 3.
[77] *Ibid.,* 7.
[78] William Bloom, *The New Age. An Anthology of Essential Writings,* London (Rider) 1991, p. xvi.

In the Christian perspective "only the light of divine Revelation clarifies the reality of sin and particularly of the sin committed at mankind's origins. Without the knowledge Revelation gives of God we cannot recognise sin clearly and are tempted to explain it as merely a development flaw, a psychological weakness, a mistake, or the necessary consequence of an inadequate social structure, etc. Only in the knowledge of God's plan for man can we grasp that sin is an abuse of freedom that God gives to created persons so that they are capable of loving him and loving one another".[79] Sin is an offense against reason, truth and right conscience; it is a failure in genuine love for God and neighbour caused by a perverse attachment to certain goods. It wounds the nature of man and injures human solidarity...[80] Sin is an offense against God... sin sets itself against God's love for us and turns our hearts away from it... Sin is thus 'love of oneself even to contempt of God'".[81]

• Are we encouraged to reject or accept suffering and death?

Some *New Age* writers view suffering as self-imposed, or as bad karma, or at least as a failure to harness one's own resources. Others concentrate on methods of achieving success and wealth (e.g. Deepak Chopra, José Silva *et al.*). In *New Age*, reincarnation is often seen as a necessary element in spiritual growth, a stage in progressive spiritual evolution which began before we were born and will continue after we die. In our present lives the experience of the death of other people provokes a healthy crisis.

Both cosmic unity and reincarnation are irreconcilable with the Christian belief that a human person is a distinct being, who lives one life, for which he or she is fully responsible: this understanding of the person puts into question both responsibility and freedom. Christians know that "in the cross of Christ not only is the redemption accomplished through suffering, but also human suffering itself has been redeemed. Christ - without any fault of his own - took on himself 'the total evil of sin'. The experience of this evil determined the incomparable extent of Christ's suffering, which

[79] *Catechism of the Catholic Church,* § 387.
[80] *Ibid.,* § 1849.
[81] *Ibid.,* § 1850.

became the price of the redemption... The Redeemer suffered in place of man and for man. Every man has his own share in the redemption, Each one is also called to share in that suffering through which the redemption was accomplished. He is called to share in that suffering through which all human suffering has also been redeemed. In bringing about the redemption through suffering, Christ has also raised human suffering to the level of the redemption. Thus each man in his suffering can also become a sharer in the redemptive suffering of Christ".[82]

• Is social commitment something shirked or positively sought after?

Much in *New Age* is unashamedly self-promotion, but some leading figures in the movement claim that it is unfair to judge the whole movement by a minority of selfish, irrational and narcissistic people, or to allow oneself to be dazzled by some of their more bizarre practices, which are a block to seeing in *New Age* a genuine spiritual search and spirituality.[83] The fusion of individuals into the cosmic self, the relativisation or abolition of difference and opposition in a cosmic harmony, is unacceptable to Christianity.

Where there is true love, there has to be a different other (person). A genuine Christian searches for unity in the capacity and freedom of the other to say 'yes' or 'no' to the gift of love. Union is seen in Christianity as communion, unity as community.

• Is our future in the stars or do we help to construct it?

The *New Age* which is dawning will be peopled by perfect, androgynous beings who are totally in command of the cosmic laws of nature. In this scenario, Christianity has to be eliminated and give way to a global religion and a new world order.

Christians are in a constant state of vigilance, ready for the last days when Christ will come again; their New Age began 2000 years ago, with Christ, who is none other than "Jesus of Nazareth; he is the Word of God made man for the salvation of all". His Holy Spirit is present and active in the hearts of individuals, in "society and

---

[82]John Paul II, *Apostolic Letter on human suffering "Salvifici doloris"* (11 February 1984), 19.
[83]Cf. David Spangler, *The New Age, op. cit.*, p. 28.

history, peoples, cultures and religions". In fact, "the Spirit of the Father, bestowed abundantly by the Son, is the animator of all".[84] *We live in the last times.*

On the one hand, it is clear that many *New Age* practices seem to those involved in them not to raise doctrinal questions; but, at the same time, it is undeniable that these practices themselves communicate, even if only indirectly, a mentality which can influence thinking and inspire a very particular vision of reality. Certainly *New Age* creates its own atmosphere, and it can be hard to distinguish between things which are innocuous and those which really need to be questioned. However, it is well to be aware that the doctrine of the Christ spread in *New Age* circles is inspired by the theosophical teachings of Helena Blavatsky, Rudolf Steiner's anthroposophy and Alice Bailey's 'Arcane School'. Their contemporary followers are not only promoting their ideas now, but also working with *New Agers* to develop a completely new understanding of reality, a doctrine known by some observers as '*New Age* truth'.[85]

---

[84] Cf. John Paul II, Encyclical Letter *Redemptoris Missio* (7 December 1990), 6, 28, and the Declaration *Dominus Iesus* (6 August 2000) by the Congregation for the Doctrine of the Faith, 12.
[85] Cf. R. Rhodes, *The Counterfeit Christ of the New Age Movement,* Grand Rapids (Baker) 1990, p. 129.

5. JESUS CHRIST OFFERS US THE WATER OF LIFE

The Church's one foundation is Jesus Christ, her Lord. He is at the heart of every Christian action, and every Christian message. So the Church constantly returns to meet her Lord. The Gospels tell of many meetings with Jesus, from the shepherds in Bethlehem to the two thieves crucified with him, from the wise elders who listened to him in the Temple to the disciples walking miserably towards Emmaus. But one episode that speaks really clearly about what he offers us is the story of his encounter with the Samaritan woman by Jacob's well in the fourth chapter of John's Gospel; it has even been described as "a paradigm for our engagement with truth".[86] The experience of meeting the stranger who offers us the water of life is a key to the way Christians can and should engage in dialogue with anyone who does not know Jesus.

One of the attractive elements of John's account of this meeting is that it takes the woman a while even to glimpse what Jesus means by the water 'of life', or 'living' water (verse 11). Even so, she is fascinated - not only by the stranger himself, but also by his message - and this makes her listen. After her initial shock at realising what Jesus knew about her ("You are right in saying 'I have no husband': for you have had five husbands, and he whom you now have is not your husband; this you said truly", verses 17-18), she was quite open to his word: "I see you are a prophet, Sir" (verse 19). The dialogue about the adoration of God begins: "You worship what you do not know; we worship what we know, for salvation is from the Jews" (verse 22). Jesus touched her heart and so prepared her to listen to what He had to say about Himself as the Messiah: "I who am speaking to you - I am he" (verse 26), prepared her to open her heart to the true adoration in Spirit and the self-revelation of Jesus as God's Anointed.

The woman "put down her water jar and hurried back to the town to tell the people" all about the man (verse 28). The remarkable

[86] Helen Bergin o.p., "Living One's Truth", in *The Furrow,* January 2000, p. 12.

effect on the woman of her encounter with the stranger made them so curious that they, too, "started walking towards him" (verse 30). They soon accepted the truth of his identity: "Now we no longer believe because of what you told us; we have heard him ourselves and we know that he really is the saviour of the world" (verse 42). They move from hearing about Jesus to knowing him personally, then understanding the universal significance of his identity. This all happens because their minds, their hearts and more are engaged.

The fact that the story takes place by a well is significant. Jesus offers the woman "a spring... welling up to eternal life" (verse 14). The gracious way in which Jesus deals with the woman is a model for pastoral effectiveness, helping others to be truthful without suffering in the challenging process of self-recognition ("he told me every thing I have done", verse 39). This approach could yield a rich harvest in terms of people who may have been attracted to the water-carrier (Aquarius) but who are genuinely still seeking the truth. They should be invited to listen to Jesus, who offers us not simply something that will quench our thirst today, but the hidden spiritual depths of 'living water'. It is important to acknowledge the sincerity of people searching for the truth; there is no question of deceit or of self-deception. It is also important to be patient, as any good educator knows. A person embraced by the truth is suddenly energised by a completely new sense of freedom, especially from past failures and fears, and "the one who strives for self-knowledge, like the woman at the well, will affect others with a desire to know the truth that can free them too".[87]

An invitation to meet Jesus Christ, the bearer of the water of life, will carry more weight if it is made by someone who has clearly been profoundly affected by his or her own encounter with Jesus, because it is made not by someone who has simply heard about him, but by someone who can be sure "that he really is the saviour of the world" (verse 42). It is a matter of letting people react in their own way, at their own pace, and letting God do the rest.

[87] *Ibid.*, p. 15.

6. POINTS TO NOTE

6.1. Guidance and sound formation are needed

Christ or Aquarius? New Age is almost always linked with 'alternatives', either an alternative vision of reality or an alternative way of improving one's current situation (magic).[88] Alternatives offer people not two possibilities, but only the possibility of choosing one thing in preference to another: in terms of religion, *New Age* offers an alternative to the Judaeo-Christian heritage. The Age of Aquarius is conceived as one which will replace the predominantly Christian Age of Pisces. *New Age* thinkers are acutely aware of this; some of them are convinced that the coming change is inevitable, while others are actively committed to assisting its arrival. People who wonder if it is possible to believe in both Christ and Aquarius can only benefit from knowing that this is very much an 'either-or' situation. "No servant can be the slave of two masters: he will either hate the first and love the second, or treat the first with respect and the second with scorn" (*Lk* 16:13). Christians have only to think of the difference between the wise men from the East and King Herod to recognise the powerful effects of choice for or against Christ. It must never be forgotten that many of the movements which have fed the *New Age* are explicitly anti-Christian. Their stance towards Christianity is not neutral, but neutralising: despite what is often said about openness to all religious standpoints, traditional Christianity is not sincerely regarded as an acceptable alternative. In fact, it is occasionally made abundantly clear that "there is no tolerable place for true Christianity", and there are even arguments justifying anti-Christian behaviour.[89] This opposition initially was confined to the rarefied realms of those who go beyond a superficial attachment to

---

[88]Cf. P. Heelas, *op. cit.*, p. 138.

[89]Elliot Miller, *A Crash Course in the New Age,* Eastbourne (Monarch) 1989, p. 122. For documentation on the vehemently anti-Christian stance of spiritualism, cf. R. Laurence Moore, "Spiritualism", in Edwin S. Gaustad (ed.), *The Rise of Adventism: Religion and Society in Mid-Nineteenth-Century America,* New York 1974, pp. 79-103, and also R. Laurence Moore, *In Search of White Crows: Spiritualism, Parapsychology, and American Culture,* New York (Oxford University Press) 1977.

New Age, but has begun more recently to permeate all levels of the 'alternative' culture which has an extraordinarily powerful appeal, above all in sophisticated Western societies.

Fusion or confusion? New Age traditions consciously and deliberately blur real differences: between creator and creation, between humanity and nature, between religion and psychology, between subjective and objective reality. The idealistic intention is always to overcome the scandal of division, but in *New Age* theory it is a question of the systematic fusion of elements which have generally been clearly distinguished in Western culture. Is it, perhaps, fair to call it '*con*fusion'? It is not playing with words to say that *New Age* thrives on confusion. The Christian tradition has always valued the role of reason in justifying faith and in understanding God, the world and the human person.[90] *New Age* has caught the mood of many in rejecting cold, calculating, inhuman reason. While this is a positive insight, recalling the need for a balance involving all our faculties, it does not justify sidelining a faculty which is essential for a fully human life. Rationality has the advantage of universality: it is freely available to everyone, quite unlike the mysterious and fascinating character of esoteric or gnostic 'mystical' religion. Anything which promotes conceptual confusion or secrecy needs to be very carefully scrutinised. It hides rather than reveals the ultimate nature of reality. It corresponds to the post-modern loss of confidence in the bold certainties of former times, which often involves taking refuge in irrationality. The challenge is to show how a healthy partnership between faith and reason enhances human life and encourages respect for creation.

Create your own reality. The widespread *New Age* conviction that one creates one's own reality is appealing, but illusory. It is crystallised in Jung's theory that the human being is a gateway from the outer world into an inner world of infinite dimensions, where each person is Abraxas, who gives birth to his own world or devours it. The star that shines in this infinite inner world is man's God and goal. The most poignant and problematic consequence of the

[90]Cf. John Paul II, Encyclical letter *Fides et Ratio* (14 September 1998), 36-48.

acceptance of the idea that people create their own reality is the question of suffering and death: people with severe handicaps or incurable diseases feel cheated and demeaned when confronted by the suggestion that they have brought their misfortune upon themselves, or that their inability to change things points to a weakness in their approach to life. This is far from being a purely academic issue: it has profound implications in the Church's pastoral approach to the difficult existential questions everyone faces. Our limitations are a fact of life, and part of being a creature. Death and bereavement present a challenge and an opportunity, because the temptation to take refuge in a westernised reworking of the notion of reincarnation is clear proof of people's fear of death and their desire to live forever. Do we make the most of our opportunities to recall what is promised by God in the resurrection of Jesus Christ? How real is the faith in the resurrection of the body, which Christians proclaim every Sunday in the creed? The *New Age* idea that we are in some sense also gods is one which is very much in question here. The whole question depends, of course, on one's definition of reality. A sound approach to epistemology and psychology needs to be reinforced - in the appropriate way - at every level of Catholic education, formation and preaching. It is important constantly to focus on effective ways of speaking of transcendence. The fundamental difficulty of all *New Age* thought is that this transcendence is strictly a self-transcendence to be achieved within a closed universe.

Pastoral resources. In Chapter 8 an indication is given regarding the principal documents of the Catholic Church in which can be found an evaluation of the ideas of *New Age*. In the first place comes the address of Pope John Paul II which was quoted in the Foreword. The Pope recognises in this cultural trend some positive aspects, such as "the search for new meaning in life, a new ecological sensivity and the desire to go beyond a cold, rationalistic religiosity". But he also calls the attention of the faithful to certain ambiguous elements which are incompatible with the Christian faith: these movements "pay little heed to Revelation", "they tend to relativise religious doctrine in favour of a vague worldview", "they often propose a pantheistic concept of God", "they replace personal responsibility to God for our actions with a sense of duty to the cosmos, thus overturning the true concept of sin and the need for redemption through Christ".[91]

6.2. Practical steps

First of all, it is worth saying once again that not everyone or everything in the broad sweep of *New Age* is linked to the theories of the movement in the same ways. Likewise, the label itself is often misapplied or extended to phenomena which can be categorised in other ways. The term *New Age* has even been abused to demonise people and practices. It is essential to see whether phenomena linked to this movement, however loosely, reflect or conflict with a Christian vision of God, the human person and the world. The mere use of the term *New Age* in itself means little, if anything. The relationship of the person, group, practice or commodity to the central tenets of Christianity is what counts.

- The Catholic Church has its own very effective *networks*, which could be better used. For example, there is a large number of pastoral centres, cultural centres and centres of spirituality. Ideally, these could also be used to address the confusion about *New Age* religiosity in a variety of creative ways, such as providing a forum for discussion and study. It must unfortunately be admitted that there are too many cases where Catholic centres of spirituality are actively involved in diffusing *New Age* religiosity in the Church. This would of course have to be corrected, not only to stop the spread of confusion and error, but also so that they might be effective in promoting true Christian spirituality. Catholic cultural centres, in particular, are not only teaching institutions but spaces for honest dialogue.[92] Some excellent specialist institutions deal with all these questions. These are precious resources, which ought to be shared generously in areas that are less well provided for.

---

[91]Cf. John Paul II, *Address to the United States Bishops of Iowa, Kansas, Missouri and Nebraska on their "Ad Limina" visit,* 28 May 1993.

[92]Cf. John Paul II, Post-Synodal Apostolic Exhortation *Ecclesia in Africa* (14 September 1995), 103. The Pontifical Council for Culture has published a handbook listing these centres throughout the world: *Catholic Cultural Centres* (3rd edition, Vatican City, 2001).

• Quite a few *New Age* groups welcome every opportunity to explain their philosophy and activities to others. Encounters with these groups should be approached with care, and should always involve persons who are capable of both explaining Catholic faith and spirituality, and of reflecting critically on *New Age* thought and practice. It is extremely important to *check the credentials* of people, groups and institutions claiming to offer guidance and information on *New Age*. In some cases what has started out as impartial investigation has later become active promotion of, or advocacy on behalf of, 'alternative religions'. Some international institutions are actively pursuing campaigns which promote respect for 'religious diversity', and claim religious status for some questionable organisations. This fits in with the *New Age* vision of moving into an age where the limited character of particular religions gives way to the universality of a new religion or spirituality. Genuine dialogue, on the other hand, will always respect diversity from the outset, and will never seek to blur distinctions in a fusion of all religious traditions.

• Some local *New Age* groups refer to their meetings as 'prayer groups'. Those people who are invited to such groups need to *look for the marks of genuine Christian spirituality*, and to be wary if there is any sort of initiation ceremony. Such groups take advantage of a person's lack of theological or spiritual formation to lure them gradually into what may in fact be a form of false worship. Christians must be taught about the true object and content of prayer - in the Holy Spirit, through Jesus Christ, to the Father - in order to judge rightly the intention of a 'prayer group'. Christian prayer and the God of Jesus Christ will easily be recognised.[93] Many people are convinced that there is no harm in 'borrowing' from the wisdom of the East, but the example of Transcendental Meditation (TM) should make Christians cautious about the prospect of committing themselves unknowingly to another religion (in this case, Hinduism), despite what TM's promoters claim about its religious neutrality. There is no problem with learning how to meditate, but

[93]Cf. Congregation for the Doctrine of the Faith, *Orationis Formas*, and § 3 above.

the object or content of the exercise clearly determines whether it relates to the God revealed by Jesus Christ, to some other revelation, or simply to the hidden depths of the self.

• Christian groups which promote *care for the earth as God's creation* also need to be given due recognition. The question of respect for creation is one which could also be approached creatively in Catholic schools. A great deal of what is proposed by the more radical elements of the ecological movement is difficult to reconcile with Catholic faith. Care for the environment in general terms is a timely sign of a fresh concern for what God has given us, perhaps a necessary mark of Christian stewardship of creation, but 'deep ecology' is often based on pantheistic and occasionally gnostic principles.[94]

• The beginning of the Third Millennium offers a real *kairos* for evangelisation. People's minds and hearts are already unusually open to reliable information on the Christian understanding of time and salvation history. Emphasising what is lacking in other approaches should not be the main priority. It is more a question of constantly revisiting the sources of our own faith, so that we can *offer a good, sound presentation of the Christian message.* We can be proud of what we have been given on trust, so we need to resist the pressures of the dominant culture to bury these gifts (cf. *Mt* 25:24-30). One of the most useful tools available is the *Catechism of the Catholic Church*. There is also an immense heritage of ways to holiness in the lives of Christian men and women past and present. Where Christianity's rich symbolism, and its artistic, aesthetical and musical traditions are unknown or have been forgotten, there is much work to be done for Christians themselves, and ultimately also for anyone searching for an experience or a greater awareness of God's presence. Dialogue between Christians and people attracted to the *New Age* will be more successful if it takes into account the appeal of what touches the emotions and symbolic language. If our task is to know, love and serve Jesus Christ, it is of paramount importance to start with a good knowledge of the Scriptures. But, most

[94]This is one area where lack of information can allow those responsible for education to be misled by groups whose real agenda is inimical to the Gospel message. It is particularly the case in schools, where a captive curious young audience is an ideal target for ideological merchandising. Cf. the *caveat* in Massimo Introvigne, *New Age & Next Age,* Casale Monferrato (Piemme) 2000, p. 277f.

of all, coming to meet the Lord Jesus in prayer and in the sacraments, which are precisely the moments when our ordinary life is hallowed, is the surest way of making sense of the whole Christian message.

• Perhaps the simplest, the most obvious and the most urgent measure to be taken, which might also be the most effective, would be *to make the most of the riches of the Christian spiritual heritage*. The great religious orders have strong traditions of meditation and spirituality, which could be made more available through courses or periods in which their houses might welcome genuine seekers. This is already being done, but more is needed. Helping people in their spiritual search by offering them proven techniques and experiences of real prayer could open a dialogue with them which would reveal the riches of Christian tradition, and perhaps clarify a great deal about *New Age* in the process.

In a vivid and useful image, one of the *New Age* movement's own exponents has compared traditional religions to cathedrals, and *New Age* to a worldwide fair. The *New Age* Movement is seen as an invitation to Christians to bring the message of the cathedrals to the fair which now covers the whole world. This image offers Christians a positive challenge, since it is always time to take the message of the cathedrals to the people in the fair. Christians need not, indeed, must not wait for an invitation to bring the message of the Good News of Jesus Christ to those who are looking for the answers to their questions, for spiritual food that satisfies, for living water. Following the image proposed, Christians must issue forth from the cathedral, nourished by word and sacrament, to bring the Gospel into every aspect of everyday life - "Go! The Mass is ended!" In his Apostolic Letter *Novo Millennio Ineunte* the Holy Father remarks on the great interest in spirituality found in the secular world of today, and how other religions are responding to this demand in appealing ways. He goes on to issue a challenge to Christians in this regard: "But we who have received the grace of believing in Christ, the revealer of the Father and the Saviour of the world, have a duty to show to what depths the relationship with Christ can lead" (n. 33). To those shopping around in the world's fair of religious proposals, the appeal of Christianity will be felt first of all in the witness of the members of the Church, in their trust, calm, patience and cheerfulness, and in their concrete love of neighbour, all the fruit of their faith nourished in authentic personal prayer.

7. APPENDIX

7.1. Some brief formulations of *New Age* ideas

William Bloom's *1992 formulation of New Age quoted in* Heelas, p. 225f.:

• All life - all existence - is the manifestation of Spirit, of the Unknowable, of that supreme consciousness known by many different names in many different cultures.

• The purpose and dynamic of all existence is to bring Love, Wisdom, Enlightenment... into full manifestation.

• All religions are the expression of this same inner reality.

• All life, as we perceive it with the five human senses or with scientific instruments, is only the outer veil of an invisible, inner and causal reality.

• Similarly, human beings are twofold creatures - with:
(i) an outer temporary personality; and
(ii) a multi-dimensional inner being (soul or higher self).

• The outer personality is limited and tends towards love.

• The purpose of the incarnation of the inner being is to bring the vibrations of the outer personality into a resonance of love.

• All souls in incarnation are free to choose their own spiritual path.

• Our spiritual teachers are those whose souls are liberated from the need to incarnate and who express unconditional love, wisdom and enlightenment. Some of these great beings are well-known and have inspired the world religions. Some are unknown and work invisibly.

• All life, in its different forms and states, is interconnected energy - and this includes our deeds, feelings and thoughts. We, therefore, work with Spirit and these energies in co-creating our reality.

• Although held in the dynamic of cosmic love, we are jointly responsible for the state of ourselves, of our environment and of all life.

• During this period of time, the evolution of the planet and of humanity has reached a point when we are undergoing a fundamental spiritual change in our individual and mass consciousness. This is why we talk of a *New Age*. This new consciousness is the result of the increasingly successful incarnation of what some people call the energies of cosmic love. This new consciousness demonstrates itself in an instinctive understanding of the sacredness and, in particular, the interconnectedness of all existence.

• This new consciousness and this new understanding of the dynamic interdependence of all life mean that we are currently in the process of evolving a completely new planetary culture.

Heelas (p. 226) Jeremy Tarcher's *'complementary formulation'*.

1. The world, including the human race, constitutes an expression of a higher, more comprehensive divine nature.
2. Hidden within each human being is a higher divine self, which is a manifestation of the higher, more comprehensive divine nature.
3. This higher nature can be awakened and can become the center of the individual's everyday life.
4. This awakening is the reason for the existence of each individual life.

David Spangler *is quoted in* Actualité des religions *n° 8, septembre 1999, p. 43, on the principal characteristics of the New Age vision, which is:*

• holistic (globalising, because there is one single reality-energy);

• ecological (earth-Gaia is our mother; each of us is a neurone of earth's central nervous system);

• androgynous (rainbow and Yin/Yang are both *New Age* symbols, to do with the complementarity of contraries, esp. masculine and feminine);

• mystical (finding the sacred in every thing, the most ordinary things);

• planetary (people must be at one and the same time anchored in their own culture and open to a universal dimension, capable of promoting love, compassion, peace and even the establishment of world government).

7.2. A Select Glossary

Age of Aquarius: each astrological age of about 2146 years is named according to one of the signs of the zodiac, but the 'great days' go in reverse order, so the current Age of Pisces is about to end, and the Age of Aquarius will be ushered in. Each Age has its own cosmic energies; the energy in Pisces has made it an era of wars and conflicts. But Aquarius is set to be an era of harmony, justice, peace, unity etc. In this aspect, *New Age* accepts historical inevitability. Some reckon the age of Aries was the time of the Jewish religion, the age of Pisces that of Christianity, Aquarius the age of a universal religion.

Androgyny: is not hermaphroditism, i.e. existence with the physical characteristics of both sexes, but an awareness of the presence in every person of male and female elements; it is said to be a state of balanced inner harmony of the *animus* and *anima*. In *New Age*, it is a state resulting from a new awareness of this double mode of being and existing that is characteristic of every man and every woman. The more it spreads, the more it will assist in the transformation of interpersonal conduct.

Anthroposophy: a theosophical doctrine originally popularised by the Croat Rudolf Steiner (1861-1925), who left the Theosophical Society after being leader of its German branch from 1902 to 1913. It is an esoteric doctrine meant to initiate people into 'objective knowledge' in the spiritual-divine sphere. Steiner believed it had helped him explore the laws of evolution of the cosmos and of humanity. Every physical being has a corresponding spiritual being, and earthly life is influenced by astral energies and spiritual essences. The *Akasha Chronicle* is said to be a 'cosmic memory' available to initiates.[95]

Channeling: psychic mediums claim to act as channels for information from other selves, usually disembodied entities living on a higher plane. It links beings as diverse as ascended masters, angels, gods, group entities, nature spirits and the Higher Self.

[95]Cf. J. Badewien, *Antroposofia,* in H. Waldenfels (ed.) *Nuovo Dizionario delle Religioni,* Cinisello Balsamo (San Paolo) 1993, 41.

Christ: in *New Age* the historical figure of Jesus is but one incarnation of an idea or an energy or set of vibrations. For Alice Bailey, a great day of supplication is needed, when all believers will create such a concentration of spiritual energy that there will be a further incarnation, which will reveal how people can save themselves... For many people, Jesus is nothing more than a spiritual master who, like Buddha, Moses and Mohammed, amongst others, has been penetrated by the cosmic Christ. The cosmic Christ is also known as christic energy at the basis of each being and the whole of being. Individuals need to be initiated gradually into awareness of this christic characteristic they are all said to have. Christ - in *New Age* terms - represents the highest state of perfection of the self.[96]

Crystals: are reckoned to vibrate at significant frequencies. Hence they are useful in self-transformation. They are used in various therapies and in meditation, visualisation, 'astral travel' or as lucky charms. From the outside looking in, they have no intrinsic power, but are simply beautiful.

Depth Psychology: the school of psychology founded by C.G. Jung, a former disciple of Freud. Jung recognised that religion and spiritual matters were important for wholeness and health. The interpretation of dreams and the analysis of archetypes were key elements in his method. Archetypes are forms which belong to the inherited structure of the human psyche; they appear in the recurrent motifs or images in dreams, fantasies, myths and fairy tales.

Enneagram: (from the Greek *ennéa* = nine + *gramma* = sign) the name refers to a diagram composed of a circle with nine points on its circumference, connected within the circle by a triangle and a hexangle. It was originally used for divination, but has become known as the symbol for a system of personality typology consisting of nine standard character types. It became popular after the publication of Helen Palmer's book *The Enneagram,*[97] but she recognises her indebtedness to the Russian esoteric thinker and

---

[96]Cf. Raúl Berzosa Martinez, *Nueva Era y Cristianismo,* Madrid (BAC) 1995, 214.
[97]Helen Palmer, *The Enneagram,* New York (Harper-Row) 1989.

practitioner G.I. Gurdjieff, the Chilean psychologist Claudio Naranjo and author Oscar Ichazo, founder of *Arica*. The origin of the enneagram remains shrouded in mystery, but some maintain that it comes from Sufi mysticism.

Esotericism: (from the Greek *esotéros* = that which is within) it generally refers to an ancient and hidden body of knowledge available only to initiated groups, who portray themselves as guardians of the truths hidden from the majority of humankind. The initiation process takes people from a merely external, superficial, knowledge of reality to the inner truth and, in the process, awakens their consciousness at a deeper level. People are invited to undertake this 'inner journey' to discover the 'divine spark' within them. Salvation, in this context, coincides with a discovery of the Self.

Evolution: in *New Age* it is much more than a question of living beings evolving towards superior life forms; the physical model is projected on to the spiritual realm, so that an immanent power within human beings would propel them towards superior spiritual life forms. Human beings are said not to have full control over this power, but their good or bad actions can accelerate or retard their progress. The whole of creation, including humanity, is seen to be moving inexorably towards a fusion with the divine. Reincarnation clearly has an important place in this view of a progressive spiritual evolution which is said to begin before birth and continue after death.[98]

Expansion of consciousness: if the cosmos is seen as one continuous chain of being, all levels of existence - mineral, vegetable, animal, human, cosmic and divine beings - are interdependent. Human beings are said to become aware of their place in this *holistic* vision of *global* reality by expanding their consciousness well beyond its normal limits. The *New Age* offers a huge variety of techniques to help people reach a higher level of perceiving reality, a way of overcoming the separation between subjects and between subjects and objects in the knowing process, concluding in total fusion of what normal, inferior, awareness sees as separate or distinct realities.

[98]Cf. document of the Argentine Episcopal Committee for Culture, *op. cit.*

Feng-shui: a form of geomancy, in this case an occult Chinese method of deciphering the hidden presence of positive and negative currents in buildings and other places, on the basis of a knowledge of earthly and atmospheric forces. "Just like the human body or the cosmos, sites are places criss-crossed by influxes whose correct balance is the source of health and life".[99]

Gnosis: in a generic sense, it is a form of knowledge that is not intellectual, but visionary or mystical, thought to be revealed and capable of joining the human being to the divine mystery. In the first centuries of Christianity, the Fathers of the Church struggled against gnosticism, inasmuch as it was at odds with faith. Some see a rebirth of gnostic ideas in much *New Age* thinking, and some authors connected with *New Age* actually quote early gnosticism. However, the greater emphasis in *New Age* on monism and even pantheism or panentheism encourages some to use the term *neo-gnosticism* to distinguish *New Age* gnosis from ancient gnosticism.

Great White Brotherhood: Mrs Blavatsky claimed to have contact with the *mahatmas*, or *masters*, exalted beings who together constitute the Great White Brotherhood. She saw them as guiding the evolution of the human race and directing the work of the Theosophical Society.

Hermeticism: philosophical and religious practices and speculations linked to the writings in the *Corpus Hermeticum,* and the Alexandrian texts attributed to the mythical *Hermes Trismegistos.* When they first became known during the Renaissance, they were thought to reveal pre-Christian doctrines, but later studies showed they dated from the first century of the christian era.[100] Alexandrian hermeticism is a major resource for modern esotericism, and the two have much in common: eclecticism, a refutation of ontological dualism, an affirmation of the positive and symbolic character of the universe, the idea of the fall and later restoration of mankind. Hermetic speculation has

---

[99] J. Gernet, in J-P. Vernant *et al., Divination et Rationalité,* Paris (Seuil) 1974, p. 55.

[100] Cf. Susan Greenwood, "Gender and Power in Magical Practices", in Steven Sutcliffe and Marion Bowman (eds.), *Beyond New Age. Exploring Alternative Spirituality,* Edinburgh (Edinburgh University Press) 2000, p. 139.

strengthened belief in an ancient fundamental tradition or a so-called *philosophia perennis* falsely considered as common to all religious traditions. The high and ceremonial forms of magic developed from Renaissance Hermeticism.

Holism: a key concept in the 'new paradigm', claiming to provide a theoretical frame integrating the entire worldview of modern man. In contrast with an experience of increasing fragmentation in science and everyday life, 'wholeness' is put forward as a central methodological and ontological concept. Humanity fits into the universe as part of a single living organism, a harmonious network of dynamic relationships. The classic distinction between subject and object, for which Descartes and Newton are typically blamed, is challenged by various scientists who offer a bridge between science and religion. Humanity is part of a universal network (eco-system, family) of nature and world, and must seek harmony with every element of this quasi-transcendent authority. When one understands one's place in nature, in the cosmos which is also divine, one also understands that 'wholeness' and 'holiness' are one and the same thing. The clearest articulation of the concept of holism is in the 'Gaia' hypothesis.[101]

Human Potential Movement: since its beginnings (Esalen, California, in the 1960s), this has grown into a network of groups promoting the release of the innate human capacity for creativity through self-realisation. Various techniques of personal transformation are used more and more by companies in management training programmes, ultimately for very normal economic reasons. Transpersonal Technologies, the Movement for Inner Spiritual Awareness, Organisational Development and Organisational Transformation are all put forward as non-religious, but in reality company employees can find themselves being submitted to an alien 'spirituality' in a situation which raises questions about personal freedom. There are clear links between Eastern spirituality and psychotherapy, while Jungian psychology and the Human Potential Movement have been very influential on Shamanism and 'reconstructed' forms of Paganism like Druidry

[101]Cf. M. Fuss, *op. cit.*, 198-199.

and Wicca. In a general sense, 'personal growth' can be understood as the shape 'religious salvation' takes in the *New Age* movement: it is affirmed that deliverance from human suffering and weakness will be reached by developing our human potential, which results in our increasingly getting in touch with our inner divinity.[102]

Initiation: in religious ethnology it is the cognitive and/or experiential journey whereby a person is admitted, either alone or as part of a group, by means of particular rituals to membership of a religious community, a secret society (e.g. Freemasonry) or a mystery association (magical, esoteric-occult, gnostic, theosophical etc.).

Karma: (from the Sanskrit root *Kri* = action, deed) a key notion in Hinduism, Jainism and Buddhism, but one whose meaning has not always been the same. In the ancient Vedic period it referred to the ritual action, especially sacrifice, by means of which a person gained access to the happiness or blessedness of the afterlife. When Jainism and Buddhism appeared (about 6 centuries before Christ), *Karma* lost its salvific meaning: the way to liberation was knowledge of the *Atman* or 'self'. In the doctrine of *samsara*, it was understood as the incessant cycle of human birth and death (Huinduism) or of rebirth (Buddhism).[103] In *New Age* contexts, the 'law of karma' is often seen as the moral equivalent of cosmic evolution. It is no longer to do with evil or suffering - illusions to be experienced as part of a 'cosmic game' - but is the universal law of cause and effect, part of the tendency of the interconnected universe towards moral balance.[104]

Monism: the metaphysical belief that differences between beings are illusory. There is only one universal being, of which every thing and every person is a part. Inasmuch as *New Age* monism includes the idea that reality is fundamentally spiritual, it is a contemporary form of pantheism (sometimes explicitly a rejection of materialism, particularly Marxism). Its claim to resolve

[102]For a brief but clear treatment of the Human Potential Movement, see Elizabeth Puttick, "Personal Development: the Spiritualisation and Secularisation of the Human Potential Movement", in: Steven Sutcliffe and Marion Bowman (eds.), *Beyond New Age. Exploring Alternative Spirituality,* Edinburgh (Edinburgh University Press) 2000, pp. 201-219.

[103]Cf. C. Maccari, *La "New Age" di fronte alla fede cristiana,* Leumann-Torino (LDC) 1994, 168.

[104]Cf. W.J. Hanegraaff, *op. cit.,* 283-290.

all dualism leaves no room for a transcendent God, so everything is God. A further problem arises for Christianity when the question of the origin of evil is raised. C.G. Jung saw evil as the 'shadow side' of the God who, in classical theism, is all goodness.

Mysticism: *New Age* mysticism is turning inwards on oneself rather than communion with God who is 'totally other'. It is fusion with the universe, an ultimate annihilation of the individual in the unity of the whole. Experience of Self is taken to be experience of divinity, so one looks within to discover authentic wisdom, creativity and power.

Neopaganism: a title often rejected by many to whom it is applied, it refers to a current that runs parallel to *New Age* and often interacts with it. In the great wave of reaction against traditional religions, specifically the Judaeo-Christian heritage of the West, many have revisited ancient indigenous, traditional, *pagan* religions. Whatever preceded Christianity is reckoned to be more genuine to the spirit of the land or the nation, an uncontaminated form of natural religion, in touch with the powers of nature, often matriarchal, magical or Shamanic. Humanity will, it is said, be healthier if it returns to the natural cycle of (agricultural) festivals and to a general affirmation of life. Some 'neo-pagan' religions are recent reconstructions whose authentic relationship to original forms can be questioned, particularly in cases where they are dominated by modern ideological components like ecology, feminism or, in a few cases, myths of racial purity.[105]

***New Age* Music:** this is a booming industry. The music concerned is very often packaged as a means of achieving harmony with oneself or the world, and some of it is 'Celtic' or druidic. Some *New Age* composers claim their music is meant to build bridges between the conscious and the unconscious, but this is probably more so when, besides melodies, there is meditative and rhythmic repetition of key phrases. As with many elements of the *New Age* phenomenon, some music is meant to bring people

---

[105]On this last, very delicate, point, see Eckhard Türk's article "Neonazismus" in Hans Gasper, Joachim Müller, Friederike Valentin (eds.), *Lexikon der Sekten, Sondergruppen und Weltanschauungen. Fakten, Hintergründe, Klärungen,* Freiburg- Basel-Wien (Herder) 2000, p. 726.

further into the *New Age* Movement, but most is simply commercial or artistic.

New Thought: a 19th century religious movement founded in the United States of America. Its origins were in idealism, of which it was a popularised form. God was said to be totally good, and evil merely an illusion; the basic reality was the mind. Since one's mind is what *causes* the events in one's life, one has to take ultimate responsibility for every aspect of one's situation.

Occultism: occult (hidden) knowledge, and the hidden forces of the mind and of nature, are at the basis of beliefs and practices linked to a presumed secret 'perennial philosophy' derived from ancient Greek magic and alchemy, on the one hand, and Jewish mysticism, on the other. They are kept hidden by a code of secrecy imposed on those initiated into the groups and societies that guard the knowledge and techniques involved. In the 19th century, spiritualism and the Theosophical Society introduced new forms of occultism which have, in turn, influenced various currents in the *New Age*.

Pantheism: (Greek *pan* = everything and *theos* = God) the belief that everything is God or, sometimes, that everything is *in* God and God is in everything (panentheism). Every element of the universe is divine, and the divinity is equally present in everything. There is no space in this view for God as a distinct being in the sense of classical theism.

Parapsychology: treats of such things as extrasensory perception, mental telepathy, telekinesis, psychic healing and communication with spirits via mediums or channeling. Despite fierce criticism from scientists, parapsychology has gone from strength to strength, and fits neatly into the view popular in some areas of the *New Age* that human beings have extraordinary psychic abilities, but often only in an undeveloped state.

Planetary Consciousness: this world-view developed in the 1980s to foster loyalty to the community of humanity rather than to nations, tribes or other established social groups. It can be seen as the heir to movements in the early 20th century that promoted a world government. The consciousness of the unity of humanity sits well with the *Gaia hypothesis*.

Positive Thinking: the conviction that people can change physical reality or external circumstances by altering their mental attitude, by thinking positively and constructively. Sometimes it is a matter of becoming consciously aware of unconsciously held beliefs that determine our life-situation. Positive thinkers are promised health and wholeness, often prosperity and even immortality.

Rebirthing: In the early 1970s Leonard Orr described rebirthing as a process by which a person can identify and isolate areas in his or her consciousness that are unresolved and at the source of present problems.

Reincarnation: in a *New Age* context, reincarnation is linked to the concept of ascendant evolution towards becoming divine. As opposed to Indian religions or those derived from them, *New Age* views reincarnation as progression of the individual soul towards a more perfect state. What is reincarnated is essentially something immaterial or spiritual; more precisely, it is consciousness, that spark of energy in the person that shares in cosmic or 'christic' energy. Death is nothing but the passage of the soul from one body to another.

Rosicrucians: these are Western occult groups involved in alchemy, astrology, Theosophy and kabbalistic interpretations of scripture. The *Rosicrucian Fellowship* contributed to the revival of astrology in the 20th century, and the *Ancient and Mystical Order of the Rosae Crucis* (AMORC) linked success with a presumed ability to materialise mental images of health, riches and happiness.

Shamanism: practices and beliefs linked to communication with the spirits of nature and the spirits of dead people through ritualised possession (by the spirits) of a shaman, who serves as a medium. It has been attractive in *New Age* circles because it stresses harmony with the forces of nature and healing. There is also a romanticised image of indigenous religions and their closeness to the earth and to nature.

Spiritualism: While there have always been attempts to contact the spirits of the dead, 19th century spiritualism is reckoned to be one of the currents that flow into the *New Age*. It developed against the background of the ideas of Swedenborg and Mesmer, and became a new kind of religion. Madame Blavatsky was a medium, and so spiritualism had a great influence on the Theosophical Society, although there the emphasis was on contact with entities from the distant past rather than people who had died only recently. Allan Kardec was influential in the spread of spiritualism in Afro-Brasilian religions. There are also spiritualist elements in some New Religious Movements in Japan.

Theosophy: an ancient term, which originally referred to a kind of mysticism. It has been linked to Greek Gnostics and Neoplatonists, to Meister Eckhart, Nicholas of Cusa and Jakob Boehme. The name was given new emphasis by the Theosophical Society, founded by Helena Petrovna Blavatsky and others in 1875. Theosophical mysticism tends to be monistic, stressing the essential unity of the spiritual and material components of the universe. It also looks for the hidden forces that cause matter and spirit to interact, in such a way that human and divine minds eventually meet. Here is where theosophy offers mystical redemption or enlightenment.

Transcendentalism: This was a 19th century movement of writers and thinkers in New England, who shared an idealistic set of beliefs in the essential unity of creation, the innate goodness of the human person, and the superiority of insight over logic and experience for the revelation of the deepest truths. The chief figure is Ralph Waldo Emerson, who moved away from orthodox Christianity, through Unitarianism to a new natural mysticism which integrated concepts from Hinduism with popular American ones like individualism, personal responsibility and the need to succeed.

Wicca: an old English term for witches that has been given to a neo-pagan revival of some elements of ritual magic. It was invented in England in 1939 by Gerald Gardner, who based it on some scholarly texts, according to which medieval European witchcraft was an ancient nature religion persecuted by Christians. Called 'the Craft', it grew rapidly in the 1960s in the United States, where it encountered 'women's spirituality'.

7.3. Key *New Age* places

Esalen: a community founded in Big Sur, California, in 1962 by Michael Murphy and Richard Price, whose main aim was to arrive at a self-realisation of being through nudism and visions, as well as 'bland medicines'. It has become one of the most important centres of the Human Potential Movement, and has spread ideas about holistic medicine in the worlds of education, politics and economics. This has been done through courses in comparative religion, mythology, mysticism, meditation, psychotherapy, expansion of consciousness and so on. Along with Findhorn, it is seen as a key place in the growth of Aquarian consciousness. The Esalen Soviet-American Institute co-operated with Soviet officials on the Health Promotion Project.

Findhorn: this holistic farming community started by Peter and Eileen Caddy achieved the growth of enormous plants by unorthodox methods. The founding of the Findhorn community in Scotland in 1965 was an important milestone in the movement which bears the label of the '*New Age*'. In fact, Findhorn "was seen as embodying its principal ideals of transformation". The quest for a universal consciousness, the goal of harmony with nature, the vision of a transformed world, and the practice of channeling, all of which have become hallmarks of the *New Age* Movement, were present at Findhorn from its foundation. The success of this community led to its becoming a model for, and/or an inspiration to, other groups, such as Alternatives in London, Esalen in Big Sur, California, and the Open Center and Omega Institute in New York".[106]

Monte Verità: a utopian community near Ascona in Switzerland. Since the end of the 19th century it was a meeting point for European and American exponents of the counter-culture in the fields of politics, psychology, art and ecology. The *Eranos* conferences have been held there every year since 1933, gathering some of the great luminaries of the *New Age*. The yearbooks make clear the intention to create an integrated world religion.[107] It is fascinating to see the list of those who have gathered over the years at Monte Verità.

[106]Cf. John Saliba, *Christian Responses to the New Age Movement. A Critical Assessment,* London, (Geoffrey Chapman) 1999, p.1.
[107]Cf. M. Fuss, *op. cit.,* 195-196.

8. RESOURCES

Documents of the Catholic Church's magisterium

John Paul II, *Address to the United States Bishops of Iowa, Kansas, Missouri and Nebraska on their "Ad Limina" visit,* 28 May 1993.

Congregation for the Doctrine of the Faith, *Letter to Bishops on Certain Aspects of Christian Meditation (Orationis Formas),* Vatican City (Vatican Polyglot Press) 1989.

International Theological Commission, *Some Current Questions Concerning Eschatology,* 1992, Nos. 9-10 (on reincarnation).

International Theological Commission, *Some Questions on the Theology of Redemption,* 1995, I/29 and II/35-36.

Argentine Bishops' Conference Committee for Culture, *Frente a una Nueva Era. Desafio a la pastoral en el horizonte de la Nueva Evangelización,* 1993.

Irish Theological Commission, *A New Age of the Spirit? A Catholic Response to the New Age Phenomenon,* Dublin 1994.

Godfried Danneels, *Au-delà de la mort: réincarnation et resurrection,* Pastoral Letter, Easter 1991.

Godfried Danneels, *Christ or Aquarius?* Pastoral Letter, Christmas 1990 (Veritas, Dublin).

Carlo Maccari, "La 'mistica cosmica' del *New Age*", in *Religioni e Sette nel Mondo* 1996/2.

Carlo Maccari, *La New Age di fronte alla fede cristiana,* Turin (LDC) 1994.

Edward Anthony McCarthy, *The New Age Movement,* Pastoral Instruction, 1992.

Paul Poupard, *Felicità e fede cristiana, Casale Monferrato (Ed. Piemme) 1992.*

Joseph Ratzinger, *La fede e la teologia ai nostri giorni,* Guadalajara, May 1996, in *L'Osservatore Romano* 27 October 1996.

Norberto Rivera Carrera, *Instrucción Pastoral sobre el New Age*, 7 January 1996.

Christoph von Schönborn, *Risurrezione e reincarnazione,* (Italian translation) Casale Monferrato (Piemme) 1990.

J. Francis Stafford, *Il movimento "New Age",* in *L'Osservatore Romano,* 30 October 1992.

Working Group on New Religious Movements (ed.), Vatican City, *Sects and New Religious Movements. An Anthology of Texts From the Catholic Church,* Washington (USCC) 1995.

Christian studies

Raúl Berzosa Martinez, *Nueva Era y Cristianismo. Entre el diálogo y la ruptura,* Madrid (BAC) 1995.

André Fortin, *Les Galeries du Nouvel Age: un chrétien s'y promène,* Ottawa (Novalis) 1993.

Claude Labrecque, *Une religion américaine. Pistes de discernement chrétien sur les courants populaires du "Nouvel Age",* Montréal (Médiaspaul) 1994.

The Methodist Faith and Order Committee, *The New Age Movement Report to Conference 1994.*

Aidan Nichols, "The *New Age* Movement", in *The Month,* March 1992, pp. 84-89.

Alessandro Olivieri Pennesi, *Il Cristo del New Age. Indagine critica,* Vatican City (Libreria Editrice Vaticana) 1999.

Ökumenische Arbeitsgruppe "Neue Religiöse Bewegungen in der Schweiz", *New Age - aus christlicher Sicht,* Freiburg (Paulusverlag) 1987.

Mitch Pacwa, SJ, *Catholics and the New Age. How Good People are being drawn into Jungian Psychology, the Enneagram and the New Age of Aquarius,* Ann Arbor MI (Servant) 1992.

John Saliba, *Christian Responses to the New Age Movement. A Critical Assessment,* London (Chapman) 1999.

Josef Südbrack, SJ, *Neue Religiosität - Herausforderung für die Christen,* Mainz (Matthias-Grünewald-Verlag) 1987 = *La nuova religiosità: una sfida per i cristiani,* Brescia (Queriniana) 1988.

"Theologie für Laien" secretariat, *Faszination Esoterik,* Zürich (Theologie für Laien) 1996.

David Toolan, *Facing West from California's Shores. A Jesuit's Journey into New Age Consciousness,* New York (Crossroad) 1987.

Juan Carlos Urrea Viera, *"New Age". Visión Histórico-Doctrinal y Principales Desafíos,* Santafé de Bogotá (CELAM) 1996.

Jean Vernette, "L'avventura spirituale dei figli dell'Acquario", in *Religioni e Sette nel Mondo* 1996/2.

Jean Vernette, *Jésus dans la nouvelle religiosité,* Paris (Desclée) 1987.

Jean Vernette, *Le New Age*, Paris (P.U.F.) 1992.

9. GENERAL BIBLIOGRAPHY

9.1. Some *New Age* books

William Bloom, *The New Age. An Anthology of Essential Writings,* London (Rider) 1991.

Fritjof Capra, *The Tao of Physics: An Exploration of the Parallels between Modern Physics and Eastern Mysticism,* Berkeley (Shambhala) 1975.

Fritjof Capra, *The Turning Point: Science, Society and the Rising Culture,* Toronto (Bantam) 1983.

Benjamin Creme, *The Reappearance of Christ and the Masters of Wisdom,* London (Tara Press) 1979.

Marilyn Ferguson, *The Aquarian Conspiracy. Personal and Social Transformation in Our Time,* Los Angeles (Tarcher) 1980.

Chris Griscom, *Ecstasy is a New Frequency: Teachings of the Light Institute,* New York (Simon & Schuster) 1987.

Thomas Kuhn, *The Structure of Scientific Revolutions,* Chicago (University of Chicago Press) 1970.

David Spangler, *The New Age Vision,* Forres (Findhorn Publications) 1980.

David Spangler, *Revelation: The Birth of a New Age,* San Francisco (Rainbow Bridge) 1976.

David Spangler, *Towards a Planetary Vision,* Forres (Findhorn Publications) 1977.

David Spangler, *The New Age*, Issaquah (The Morningtown Press) 1988.

David Spangler, *The Rebirth of the Sacred,* London (Gateway Books) 1988.

9.2. Historical, descriptive and analytical works

Christoph Bochinger, *"New Age" und moderne Religion: Religionswissenschaftliche Untersuchungen,* Gütersloh (Kaiser) 1994.

Bernard Franck, *Lexique du Nouvel-Age,* Limoges (Droguet-Ardant) 1993.

Hans Gasper, Joachim Müller and Friederike Valentin, *Lexikon der Sekten, Sondergruppen und Weltanschauungen. Fakten, Hintergründe, Klärungen,* updated edition, Freiburg-Basel-Vienna (Herder) 2000. See, *inter alia,* the article "*New Age*" by Christoph Schorsch, Karl R. Essmann and Medard Kehl, and "Reinkarnation" by Reinhard Hümmel.

Manabu Haga and Robert J. Kisala (eds.), "The *New Age* in Japan", in *Japanese Journal of Religious Studies,* Fall 1995, vol. 22, numbers 3 & 4.

Wouter Hanegraaff, *New Age Religion and Western Culture. Esotericism in the Mirror of Nature,* Leiden-New York-Köln (Brill) 1996. This book has an extensive bibliography.

Paul Heelas, *The New Age Movement. The Celebration of the Self and the Sacralization of Modernity*, Oxford (Blackwell) 1996.

Massimo Introvigne, *New Age & Next Age,* Casale Monferrato (Piemme) 2000.

Michel Lacroix, *L'Ideologia della New Age,* Milano (Il Saggiatore) 1998.

J. Gordon Melton, *New Age Encyclopedia,* Detroit (Gale Research Inc) 1990.

Elliot Miller, *A Crash Course in the New Age,* Eastbourne (Monarch) 1989.

Georges Minois, *Histoire de l'athéisme,* Paris (Fayard) 1998.

Arild Romarheim, *The Aquarian Christ. Jesus Christ as Portrayed by New Religious Movements,* Hong Kong (Good Tiding) 1992.

Hans-Jürgen Ruppert, *Durchbruch zur Innenwelt. Spirituelle Impulse aus New Age und Esoterik in kritischer Beleuchtung,* Stuttgart (Quell Verlag) 1988.

Edwin Schur, *The Awareness Trap. Self-Absorption instead of Social Change,* New York (McGraw Hill) 1977.

Rodney Stark and William Sims Bainbridge, *The Future of Religion. Secularisation, Revival and Cult Formation,* Berkeley (University of California Press) 1985.

Steven Sutcliffe and Marion Bowman (eds.), *Beyond the New Age. Exploring Alternative Spirituality,* Edinburgh (Edinburgh University Press), 2000.

Charles Taylor, *Sources of the Self. The Making of the Modern Identity,* Cambridge (Cambridge University Press) 1989.

Charles Taylor, *The Ethics of Authenticity,* London (Harvard University Press) 1991.

Edênio Valle s.v.d., "Psicologia e energias da mente: teorias alternativas", in *A Igreja Católica diante do pluralismo religioso do Brasil (III).* Estudos da CNBB n. 71, São Paulo (paulus) 1994.

World Commission on Culture and Development, *Our Creative Diversity. Report of the World Commission on Culture and Development,* Paris (UNESCO) 1995.

M. York, "The *New Age* Movement in Great Britain", in *Syzygy. Journal of Alternative Religion and Culture,* 1:2-3 (1992) Stanford CA.